THE

ZEA

MEX10

D1

*Wisconsin Studies in American Autobiography*

WILLIAM L. ANDREWS
General Editor

# THE
# ZEA
# MEXICAN
# DIARY

7 Sept 1926 – 7 Sept 1986

*Kamau*
*Brathwaite*

With a Foreword by

Sandra Pouchet Paquet

The University of Wisconsin Press

*Wisconsin Studies in American Autobiography*
WILLIAM L. ANDREWS
General Editor


A list of titles in Wisconsin Studies in
American Autobiography follows page 215


The University of Wisconsin Press
114 North Murray Street
Madison, Wisconsin 53715


3 Henrietta Street
London WC2E 8LU, England

5   4   3   2   1


Printed in the United States of America

Library of Congress Cataloging-in-Publication Data
Brathwaite, Kamau [Edward].
The Zea Mexican diary / Kamau Brathwaite: with a foreword by
Sandra Pouchet Paquet.
230 p.     cm. —(Wisconsin studies in American autobiography)
ISBN 0-299-13640-X
1. Brathwaite, Edward—Diaries. 2. Authors, Jamaican—20th
century—Diaries. 3. Brathwaite, Edward—Marriage. 4. Cancer—
Patients—Biography. 5. Authors' wives—Biography.
6. Brathwaite, Doris Monica. I. Title. II. Series.
PR9320.9.B68Z475        1993
818—dc20
[B]          92-56924

# FOREWORD

Kamau Brathwaite is foremost among modern Caribbean writers in versatility and scale of influence.[1] He is a formidable poet who has revitalized the geopsychic space of Caribbean poetry since the publication of his first volume of poetry, *Rights of Passage*, in 1967. He is the author of two outstanding trilogies and several other volumes of poetry that have redefined the meaning and centrality of Africa in Caribbean life and letters. His achievement as a poet has been complemented by major contributions in other areas as well. For Kamau Brathwaite is also a renowned historian and critic: his impact on Caribbean letters and, by extension, on Diasporan and American studies is to be measured in each of these areas, and in his projection of an aesthetic personality that has rejected disciplinary boundaries and achieved the transformative vision of poet, critic, and cultural historian combined.

Brathwaite achieved international recognition as a poet with the publication of his first trilogy, *Rights of Passage* (1967), *Masks* (1968), and *Islands* (1969). The trilogy, subsequently published as a single volume entitled *The Arrivants* (1973), registers the rootlessness and restlessness of the Caribbean psyche in contradictory impulses of migration and return. Brathwaite's trilogy trans-

[1] Kamau Brathwaite has also published under the names Edward Kamau Brathwaite and L. E. Brathwaite.

v

formed the values of Cesaire's negritude into an epic quest for the submerged, unrecognized, and unexamined dimensions of the African psyche in the Caribbean. *Rights of Passage* surveys the familiar trek of Caribbean peoples to the great urban centers of Europe and North America as a process of psychic disassembly that is arrested in the second volume of the trilogy. In *Masks,* the transformative experience for the rootless, alienated Caribbean soul occurs in the recovery of Africa as an ancestral landscape for modern Caribbean consciousness. The artistic and intellectual center of *Islands* and, indeed, of the trilogy as a whole, is the simultaneous demystification and mythification of Africa as the historical and symbolic core of the Caribbean psyche.

In his autobiographical essay "Timehri,"[2] Brathwaite arrogates the role of houngan in a broadly conceived Ceremony of Souls:

> In the Caribbean, whether it be African or Amerindian, the recognition of an ancestral landscape with the folk or aboriginal culture involves the artist and participants in a journey into the past and hinterland which is at the same time a movement of possession into present and future. Through this movement of possession we become ourselves, truly our own creators, discovering word for object, image for word (42).

Brathwaite saw himself as the creator of a language, historical and poetical, that would unify the Caribbean community. He sought to infuse the strength of his vast experience and knowledge of the world in a willful Caribbeanization of the word. From early in his career, Brathwaite grappled directly with the English language as a

[2] Published in *Is Massa Day Dead?,* edited by Orde Coombs (New York: Anchor, 1974), 29–46.

psychic prison and with inherited speech genres as composing a site of struggle and resistance. Brathwaite, like Frantz Fanon and George Lamming before him, concluded that: "It was in langauge that the slave was perhaps most successfully imprisoned by his master, and it was in his (mis)-use of it that he most effectively rebelled" (*Creole Society* 237). His poetry characteristically subverts the inherited rhythms and forms of colonial English to embody and project those of Caribbean life.

Kamau Brathwaite's wide-ranging cultural project of recovery and affirmation, in its manifold dimensions, altered the intellectual landscape of the postcolonial Caribbean in the seventies. His reputation as the Caribbean's foremost cultural historian and cultural theorist was established with a series of discourse-defining publications on the acculturative and interculturative dimensions of Caribbean societies, most notably *Folk Culture of the Slaves of Jamaica* (1970), *The Development of Creole Society in Jamaica 1770 to 1820* (1971), *Contradictory Omens: Cultural Diversity and Integration in the Caribbean* (1974), and *Our Ancestral Heritage: A Bibliography of the English-speaking Caribbean* (1977). The scale of Brathwaite's impact on Caribbean letters broadened steadily into the eighties with the publication of *History of the Voice: The Development of Nation Language in Anglophone Caribbean Poetry* (1984) and *Roots: Literary Criticism* (1986).

Brathwaite's second trilogy, *Mother Poem* (1977), *Sun Poem* (1982), and *X/Self* (1988), is arguably more autobiographical in its symbolic structures than his first trilogy. But Brathwaite's characteristic autobiographical poise is still the sweeping collectivization of personal experience. In *The Arrivants,* his private odyssey from the Caribbean to England to West Africa and back to the Caribbean is written as the collective Caribbean/Diasporan condition. In the second trilogy, the geopsychic space of the Caribbean demarcated in *The Arrivants* is gendered as well as racialized; personal experience of mother, father, and native landscape is metamorphorized to reflect the collective inheritance of a people and a culture. The process obscures and mystifies the autobiographical base of both trilogies, even as it clarifies and intensifies historical consciousness.

*The Zea Mexican Diary* stands in marked contrast to the previously published work of Kamau Brathwaite. In his multifaceted career, Brathwaite has projected the public persona of an individual talent utterly invested in the postcolonial project of regional cultural reconstruction, of "the self without ego, without I, without arrogance" ("Timehri" 35). *The Zea Mexican Diary* projects a different aesthetic personality: the persona of the public poet as cultural historian and critic on a seamless mission of recovery and affirmation of the African heart of the Caribbean appears instead a lonely individual talent, isolated and alienated from the community in which he had encased and defined himself. The public poet, who sought to embody, in his life and work, the diasporan quest for wholeness on his return to the Caribbean after eight years spent working with the Ministry of Education in Ghana (1955–1962), projects an aesthetic sensibility shattered by the circumstances surrounding the death of his beloved wife, Doris Monica, some three months after she was diagnosed as terminally ill with cancer. Brathwaite's cultural project had barely begun when he met and married Doris while on a long leave in

Barbados. She returned to Ghana with him and assumed active partnership in his life's work. Her dedication to Brathwaite's momentous cultural project remained an unrecorded and unwritten dimension of his life's work until the publication of her exhaustive bibliography, *EKB: His Published Prose and Poetry 1948–1986* (1986), in the year of her death, and the poet's passionate account of the circumstances surrounding her death in *The Zea Mexican Diary*.

*The Zea Mexican Diary* makes public a different side of Kamau Brathwaite. Leadership gives way to grief and lamentation in an unparalleled public examination of hitherto unrevealed aspects of self, of self and community, of the author's intimate relationship with his wife, and, by extension, of women's role in a male-defined cultural enterprise. *The Zea Mexican Diary* records the tormented end of a life-sustaining relationship that moves from disbelief and denial to rage and withdrawal and, finally, to acceptance and a measured joy and celebration in the lived-life. It celebrates "the perfect wife of/for the poet." It is also ritual lamentation and petitionary commemoration: "God has come to punish me for not cherishing enough." In *The Zea Mexican Diary*, ritual expressions of grief acquire new aesthetic characteristics as published diary and record of events as they occurred. It is intimate and yet it houses the ultimate expression of cosmic will. *The Zea Mexican Diary* is a rite of passage, a truly communicant ritual in which an anguished continuum of transition occurs.

*The Zea Mexican Diary* includes nine extracts from a diary Kamau Brathwaite started when he learned that his wife was terminally ill, nine extracts from letters he wrote to his sister Mary Morgan in an attempt to reopen lines of

ix

communication across the breach created by Doris's suffering and death, a statement written by the author on the night of her death and read at her Thanksgiving service by Edward Baugh, and a letter written by Ayama, which is interwoven with the author's meditations on the words and the Thanksgiving service that occasioned them. Though the diary and the letters originally were not intended for publication, the completeness and depth of aesthetization in the final form of *The Zea Mexican Diary* confirms the aesthetic contemplation immanent in any work of art.

The text coheres in its multifarious parts thematically and architecturally. In its formal aspects, the ritual of grief and lamentation is sculpted on the page with great meticulousness. Lines and fonts are varied to achieve rhythmic effects, to mirror emotional states, and for thematic emphasis. The solitary selfconfessional core of the narrative is subsumed in its polyphonic design, in its many-voicedness, and in its intimations of restored community beyond the alienation and marginalization imposed by grief and loss. It is interesting that Kamau Brathwaite chooses the circumscribed autobiographical space of the diary as personal communication to restage his changing emotional states around Doris's illness and death. Though it is elegaic in mood and function, in its insistence on names, places, and the sequence of events, *The Zea Mexican Diary* retains the implacable historicity of a memorial carved in stone. It shapes a compelling representation of the tormented end of a life-sustaining relationship that slowly and painfully moves beyond lamentation and recrimination towards acceptance and reconnection. It is a wonderfully concrete self-reflexive meditation on change and continuance framed by the philosophical directives of the *I Ching,* "If he do repent of former errors, there will be good fortune in his going forward."

*The Zea Mexican Diary* asks important questions about the culture of death, about the nature of community and Doris's place in it in life and death. The emphasis is on journey rather than arrival, on the intertransmutation of essence, ideal, and materiality into a single immortal form. Doris's death becomes a creative act. Grief becomes a process of creation. *The Zea Mexican Diary* expresses pain and grief and love in a way that is restorative without the customary platitudes. The moral imperative of this new aesthetic privileges private expression of grief in a public forum. All grief cannot be expressed in the customary public rituals, when so much of it is felt in such a private, lonely space.

University of Miami                    SANDRA POUCHET PAQUET

# Kamau Brath-waite

# THE

# ZEA

# MEXICAN

# DIARY

7 Sept 1926 - 7 Sept 1986

*New York Feb 93. the Stark version*

All during these events I hear Ken Boothe,
the Jamaican 'pop' singer, singing this what at first appears to be a typical love song
but as Things Went Forward
I came to realize that it is also an xtremely poignant song of loss & mourning that
won't let me go - love & loss being so strangely twined.
For a long time, though, I felt I shouldn't use it but in recent months [feb 93]
it has returned like the nightingale to haunt me
So I must release it/written here from memory w/ respects to the composer & singer

if there is someone you know
that won't let you go
and taking it/for granted

you may lose them one day
someone takes them away
and you won't/hear a word they say

i would give everything i own
give up my life my heart my home
just to have you/back again

Ken Boothe/David Gaites

# Note of Thanks & Acknowledgement

Respects due to Gordon Rohlehr who signalled the first encouragement of a document intended at first fr yr eyes only; to Sandra Pouchet Paquet who not only xpressed faith in what I had done & how I had done it but placed ZMD in the hands of a sympathetic publisher & has agreed to write the Introduction; to Jere for critically & lovingly reading the second draft & confirming the way forward; Deanna Heaven for converting that second ts into the 'double space' the publishers required & for discovering the font that has become central to this production and for helping to convert her ts to my Sycoraxian 'video' (whose evident idio or idiot/syncrasies are all mine); to Dream Chad for checking the 'video' (helping you to be able to read it!); and my publisher for patience & taking the step forward into 'video' (the unventional stylemetre or manner in which I have presented this Diary – the 'video style' I now use for my work). Thanks too to Ken Boothe for singing his song & allowing me to re/produce it here

**W**hen EKB came face to face with the  unimaginable news

**26 May that his wife** Doris Monica

**was terminally ill he started an ms diary which he kept**

**helplessly & spasmodically until she died on her birthday**

7 September **after which to the day of her** Tree Planting 12 October

**during what he calls** The Time of Salt **he wrote a series of**

Letters to Mary Morgan **his sister**


**Attached are nine X**tracts **from the** Diary **& nine from the** Letters

**Bridging them are the words EKB wrote the very midnight of her**

**death/ which were read for him at her** Thanksgiving  Service

**at the University Chapel Mona**

15 September **by** Edward Baugh

**and a letter written outside that**

**Chapel Service**

**that same afternoon by** Aya **daughter of** Obatala

# The Second K'un
# Oppression

```
——————    ——————
————————————
————————————
——————    ——————
————————————
——————    ——————
```

The first line, divided, shows its subject with bare buttocks straitened under the stump of a tree. He enters a dark valley, and for three years has no prospect (of deliverance)

The second line, undivided, shows its subject straitened amidst the wine and viands, There comes to him anon the red knee-covers (of the ruler). It will be well for him (to maintain his sincerity as) in sacrificing Active operations (on his part) will lead to evil, but he will be free from blame

The third line, [un]-divided, shows its subject straitened before a (frowning) rock. He lays hold of thorns. He enters his palace, and does not see his wife. There will be evil . . .

The fourth line. . . divided, shows its subject proceeding very slowly (to help the subject of the first line), who is straitened by the carriage adorned with metal in front of him. There will be occasion for regret, but the end will be good . . .

The fifth line, undivided, shows its subject with his nose and feet cut off. He is straitened by (his ministers in their) scarlet aprons. . . It will be well for him to be (as sincere) as in sacrificing (to spiritual beings)

The sixth line, divided, shows its subject straitened, as if bound with creepers or in a high and dangerous position, and saying (to himself), 'If I move, I shall repent it.' If he do repent of former errors, there will be good fortune in his going forward

**I**

# Irish Town.

# 1

# 3O May 1986

The Third Day after the News. It is five in the early morning, end of May, the month of my birthday*
Dawn light about to come. Bird calls thru the rain
[This was the time of the May/June flood-rains that claim
ed a dozen lives in Jamaica & $millions in property dam
age. We could not get out of our partly flooded Irish Tn
house for some three days] All this end of May has
been rain, soft mist up here in the mountains. A
beautiful time, the at-last broken drought On Tuesday phone call from the office: **Dr Morgan wants
to see you. It's about yr wife.** D, complaining
of a cough & being v tired, had gone down to see
him that morning & had not yet returned. She came back before I left, taking ages it seemed to get
out of the car. I thought he'd told her what it was
about. But he'd said nothing to her. **He couldnt**

---

*The whole thing/ our lives to her death/ began in the month of my
birth & ended on the day of hers

19

He showed me two **X**/ray pictures of her chest. Th

(e) first one, only five weeks ago, after she'd had

the ?stroke at Penlyne, was black & strong. The se-

cond one was riddled w/ pale circles. All he could

say in sympathy/compassion (?compensation) was

I'm very sorry I'm really very sorry It was as if a

clock was ticking silence in the moon And I couldn't

believe what I was seeing hearing meaning. Was

this true? was this real? was this happening? was

there hope? I mean what now cd we do/ wd we do

And he was still shaking his head w/ all the time

of that afternoon like it was tickin away tickin a-

way tickin away Was there any way out? And

there wasnt a direct answer Only the I'm really

very sorry as if he had fallen against the wall &

only the two of us there in that dark very bright

room & there was nothing he cd do & there was

nothing we cd do & we said nothing more as if

the less said the less might it happen **X**cept that

I shouldnt say anything shouldnt say any-

thing yet to her Because it wd probably br-

eak her [kill her was the word he actually used] &

20

the sense, somehow *(did he speak out these terribles)* that she didn't have much time left neither . . .


## 2

In the middle of her life In the middle of our year
(s). So many plans. So much building. Because she
was a builder. A creator. Which makes it even more
difficult to understand. What happens to Penlyne?
What happens to the road to the house she dream
(s) of? What happens to the library work w/ which she is so deeply involved? What will happen
when she hears, when she knows? For Sun Bryan
to come to talk about plans for Penlyne & to know
that she won't be there anymore Can't be there anymore Will there be any point in continuing these
things? For whom will we be building now/ after to
day? She has no child, no future of her own flesh
& had never spoken of adoption. The building, I
think, was her child, her future. Her love.  Her energy [though I may be wrong . . .]

# 3

Very few people will know what an **X**traordinary person this is. To the outside she appeared no dou bt quiet & conventional/ quite the opposite: as the flood of tributes from all over were to so positively assert

# 4

The first wonderful thing about her is her **MORAL ITY**. She believes in marriage, in one man one wife On this level she was never too comfortable w/ certain things [polygamy, for one] in Africa though she saw their point (am not **X**pressing this v well); ack= nowledged/accepted our culture there. She believes as the song goes in Love in the responsibility to Vo ws & I know I hurt her deeply many times . . . She lived a good clean healthy 'yoga' life And as she says was never sick in all her growing up Was ne ver ill in all the 25+ yrs I knew her And now for a strong beautiful generous woman to be so struck down like this/ with this - and is no consolation that dem say Those who the gods love . . .

Her GENEROSITY is the next thing. She hardly ever had an unkind word or thought for anybody. She cd always see w/ them, for them. Something I was hardly ever able to do [and didnt even have to/ since she was always so completely here]. Above all she was generous w/ me! ?Accepted perhaps because she so understood, I think (hope) my weaknesses and because I hope (think) she felt that these 'weaknesses' far outweighed what she thought (I hope) were far more important qualities & commitments: she utterly & absolutely supported EKB the poet//writer - there cd be no question of her committment to that & through that to the whole community & environment of Caribbean literature, culture & development . . .

Her COURAGE. All these, MORALITY & GENEROSITY were/are reflections — of the same inner RADIANCE/ her NAM. You felt safe w/ her; cd depend on her.

23

She was as many were to say a FAITHFUL WIFE.
Also a faithful PERSON  True to herself & therefore
fear/less. I mean she put on that helmet/ rode a
motorbike thru London RUSH HOUR TRAFFIC/ fell
down once in the middle of it all but went back
out the next day as if nothing had happened tho
she was human enough to admit that she was frightened.  This is the same woman therefore who cd
put herself between me & the red-eye driver w/ the
knife who came one afternoon onto our College Common porch, accusing me of passing him in my car
in the rain & plashing him & him passengers
- when him own cyar had no windows or rath
er had ALL WINDOWS so all the storm was coming
in? Something like how one day at RoundHouse
[native home Bay St Btown Bdos] on our back steps,
a limb of our duncks tree was like about to fall-
down on me when my mother (then 70 yrs of age) threw
herself between the branch & me trying to hold
it back, I remember, even before I could move . .

24

And on that midday stroke at Penlyne, how tho
she couldnt talk, she struggled thru her teeth &
violent gesticulation to make me understand that I
shd not forget to pay Sun Bryan

[It was this COURAGE, then, that was to take her
through this illness & finally like the osun bird
in Yoruba imagination, transform/transcend it into
miracle - not the one I had hoped for - but miracle of self: the osun bird free of the thicks & thorn
(s) . . . the miracle of her outer/inner BEAUTY]

# 5

On this third day of rain, she sleeps upstairs, still
not knowing. But she is already much weaker. Mu
ch more fragile. Standing before her yesterday, she
seemed shorter. Have started driving her to work,
esp since it is [University] vac now. I want to hold
her touch her touch her touch her I wish by doing
this I could heal her bring her back. Am terrified

at what will happen How will she take it? The suffering she'll have to go through. How long? How
long? To know & still be able to say/ do nothing.
This is perhaps the most terrible thing of all. To
be so helpless in the face of time . . . She has to
ld me recently, esp after the second 'stroke', that
she don't intend to go back into hospital. That she won't
like to drag on if something else happened But I don't
think either of us cd have **X**pected this And she
doesn't even know yet! Will God give us strength?

# 6

I sit on the edge of tears. I suppose when the doctor said not to tell her yet, he was also giving me
chance - & Mary chance - to come to terms w/ the
terminal - even if I for one will never accept it . .
. O how I wish I was not writing this . . . Dint ev-
en wish to start, as if in starting this I am admit
ing it.   Like yesterday when I turned back to
write her name on the Dedication to **X**/self: for

**Mexican With all my love.** Like I was letting fare-
well in . . .

Tues Wed Th esp Wed & Th. There was **hope**. *Perhaps the picture was wrong!* Impossible of course.
Perhaps the doctors could do something. But look
at the spread of the disease & its speed

The rain has stopped. The light of the Third Day
is here. She sleeps upstairs. Lord, why do we love?
Why do we break our hearts? Just when we were
getting closer Just when I was coming to appreciate her cherish her more Just when I was beginning
to understand what **love** means. . . When she eventually **looks** at me with that knowledge. . .
What then?

[In anycase I had always assumed that if anybody 'went', it wd be me - 4 yrs younger than her
but the 'weaker sex'. Much weaker. And I was giving her my manuscripts & asking her to keep the
various 'versions' & dinning into her how she wd

have to speak/speak up for me/the work when I was
gone & dealin wid all dem 'unfair critic' dem . . .
like Valerie Eliot - Eliot wife - one a dem great literary windows . . . ]


# 7
## Sat 31 May 6am

I go on hoping for the miracle. Fool myself I supp
ose, that her time is surely not yet. And yet I remember how Kim Laurence another beautiful woman, went. And Shirley Aub up here in Irish Town
And Hazel Clarke long ago now And Gwennie Arm-
strong in Barbados.  These most beautiful most lov
ed of women seem to go first & fast from us so help
lessly so sudden . . .

Yesterday she went to work & had to wait for me
almost 3 hours at the Tourist Board because the
electrician up here hadn't finished what he came
to do. Two hours he said & took five! And work-

ed in the rain. I went down in the Niva for her &
she was waiting there out front, watching the rain

This morning, still raining, the house flooding,
she said she wasn't so tired now, but that she wished the doctor would give her some antibiotic for
the cough . . .


10 am
Rain Rain Rain . . . She made a tour of the grounds
in her straw hat then came in to help mop up my
study & clean out the computer room

Now she is tired & is back in bed. I sit in the room
downstairs & try not to hear that now steady steady cough/ing . . .


PS

During the clean-up this morning she came in to ki
ss me 'for being so strangely co-operative . . .' and
told Mary that these days I don't seem to ever leave her
side . . . 'Mr Brathwaite has become so attentive!' she
says, smiling . . . and still not knowing/still not knowing how I lie awake each night next to her/next
to her/ near near nearest to her/ listening to each br
eath in those nightmare **X**/ray lungs toiling toiling away/ fearing to hear some like nuclear disaster & wishing that it cd be me instead of her/ me
instead of her/ me instead of her . . . going up up
up in the dark & horror of the **X**tinction in those lungs I had seen in the picture

# 8
# Sunday 8 June

All this takes place at the time of the CHERNOBYL
NUCLEAR DISASTER near Kiev in the Soviet Union.
First Western Reports [honest/Free Press etc etc] put
the death toll at 20,000 The official Soviet count

is like 12! But they have found 'hot spots of radiation' outside the official disaster area . . .

Ever since the doc's news there has been rain here in Ja: 2 weeks of ruin that has claimed *30 lives* (& is still continuing) w/ *40,000 people they say homeless in S Clarendon alone* Roads gone Bridges wash away etc etc etc Right here at home the mud came down the hill down the front steps into the house and all her newly planted garden beds are wash'd away What a metaphor for what must be going on inside her And she still hasn't yet been told . .

# 9

# 11 June

3 WEEKS NOW. Since **Tues 27 May** and she still doesn't know. Still hasn't been told . . . She goes on planning planting looking forward. Though wondering what is wrong. Though not wondering so much aloud to me anymore. Guessing? Suspecting?

Knowing it deep down perhaps? Not able to stay awake at night at all now. Nodding off in her chair by 7 o'clock though still insisting she going out to work tomorrow & I bound to the doctor's silence & can't say anything as I watch her . . . can't give no 'good reason' to stop her tell her why she shouldn't . . . And she feels already frail. And looks smaller And her features have somehow changed, I think . . . All the strength & power draining away . . .

Yesterday she made out my Students Xam List on the computer - on her belov:ed Kaypro, using a programme she had designed herself. It had some buggs in it. And she worked away at that. And worked away at that. But she was tired. And admitted it. And I encouraged her to take rests

Today she hopes to finish it. Add in the names of the students . . .

# 10

[In her lost days there were three things she kept near her with her always. The Kaypro (which poor darling she has no strength for now, though it was there because she hoped to show me how to use it. All her work + the *Savacou* accounts & subscription lists are locked up in its secrets); her blanket (which has become a kind of Comforter); & the **X**tra-crafted Sony radio I gave her couple years ago (this was the very very last to 'go' to be 'abandoned' . . . though it remained by her' at the side of her bed' until the very end . . . )]

**II**

# Irish Town.[2]

# 1

**Mary hopes for a miracle.** But there is no such thing as 'hopeful error' in scientific medicine. But I went along w/ her until this morning when I woke up with my mind at the deathbed (or nearly) & then coming back up here alone & wondering what to do w/ her clothes & imagining having to go through the papers etc You can say that my mind is slowly coming to accept it. And at the same time she was lying there & I embraced her still trying to hold her to keep her. Like last night. By nine, watching her helplessly nodding off in the chair, so vulnerable. So alone, too, it seemed so far away - I knowin (g) what she didn't know about her own life & possible death & not being able to reach her. touch her. heal her. I brought her to bed, again w/ the thought w/ the hope that if I cd put my arms around her round her round her round her it might save her . . .

## 2

No one wants to die esp when there seems no reason for it. And when the sudden spread of second-
ary cancer - spiderwebs of metastases - through-
out the body is the last thing on your mind. I
mean you wd think that there are signals - that
doctors wd spot these things

## 3

Yesterday I Ching gave Hope. The hexagram read
FU RETURNING & gave the impression that in 7 days
there wd be easy passage . . . But perhaps it gave
me (as the I Ching often does) what I wanted to hear.
The harsh reality of the Second K'un remains . . .

## 4

I am so lonely here. But she will be so much more
so when she knows - and worse - when she feels.

When the disease begins to **destroy** & make her suffer. **No** one will be able to help her then. To follow her into that valley ... **But why why why why should it be her???**

# 5

[I give thanks that I was wrong about this When at last she came to know, she created **new life** a new life/ a new, as it seems, serenity of **caritas** & light & gave, as many said, a **shining** **X**ample (that's the word everyone used) of hope & confidence ... how she wd call me in th (e) middle of the night or morning to show me files/ what was in there/ where things were/ what did they mean etc writing it all down (or as much, as it turned out, as she cd) ... four sighting ... going farward ... ]

# 6

The cough, as it turned out, became less & less of a 'problem'. Hugh Wynter & Sheila, discussing, at my urge, the possibilities (I simply & desperately want-ed to know what was happening to her What was GOING ON INSIDE THERE What shd I X/PECT - wasn't this natural? - and WHAT SHD I DO) had said yes

# HAEMORRHAGE

for one . . . Why is it that doctors are so vague, ne ver use language; so anxious, it seems, to 'bedside' to avoid . . . Marina Omowale said this is their way . . . preparing me to do what I have to do/ since is only me who cd/wd/have to do it . . . the burden & responsibility of my love . . .

But the cough diminished/ went practically away . . . it was the sudden appearance of the rhabid/ sarcoma manifested in the thighs . . . which she ?fooled herself for a long time was 'muscle strain' ('muscle bound' . . . she of all people!) & again some of the docs went along w/ this . . . appear to/ any

42

way . . . which really damaged her/ brought the pain and the - what hurt her most - *restriction of her movement* - if only I cd move . . . if only I cd move

And it was here I couldn't help her . . . for the lungs, I was in touch w/ Betelgeuse . . . beating there in the heart of the cold fury of Orion . . . whenever she coughed or seemed in danger, I wd bring that throbbing nebula into the very centre of my head my heart my hurt & hold off . . . it seemed . . . whatever was going on wrong in there in there in there . . . I came to reach far out far out in space into the very wound & darkness of our/selves out there/ far out/ deep down in/side . . . out there . . . And it seemed as if I might win . . . *was winning* . . . if only I cd find the strength . . . the certitude . . . that power of the miracle . . . ice cold heat . . . lava of icicle . . . pure freedom of my very breath/ our breathing origines . . .

# But for the miracle to be . . . it must be . . . beyond contamination

## 7
## Sunday 15 June

I wake up early/ she still sleeping/ looking for a sign . . . Today, surely. something shd happen, there shd be some relief, some way out into hope perhaps, out of the bad dream/ wake up into better days . . .

About 8 o'clock, Mr Reid, our soft-spoken soft-stepping plangent neighbour who has a sick wife that D takes down to the doctor from time to time [is this same Mr Reid who's going perform that ritual at her Tulip Tree Planting later . . . in September] arrived outside my window (I was working on Tony Bland's poems on the Eagle) with an infant [his 18 month-young grand-daughter] in his arms.  The poor child had been burnt [all over her chest & belly with the white flesh squall & raw & glowing] Pulled down a hot blinding cup of tea onto her tiny living bosom. D, who was awake by then, called out to hear what was happening & right away,  even in her condition, wanted to take them down to town . . . worried that if I went I might not have enough time to finish my [first Annual] Report for the Citizens Association

I take the child & mother to UWI Casualty. For the whole half-hour journey the little infant made not a sound not a single cry/complaint, cradled in her mother's arms wrapped round/ protected from the bruising air by a white gentle cotton cloth & all her mother's love, staring quietly out at us thru dry & very luminous black eyes

En route the mother said Mr Bratwaite, only children of the poor gets burns . . .

**8**

# Fri 4 July

*On this angry muggy day, grey, you can't see the blue. She went w/ Hope Francis to see Sheila Wynter having been told by me last Tuesday what wa (s) happening*

[I had blurted it out - kind of - after a vi sit to one of the specialists who again we nt through the ?humane charade of pretending (to her) that nothing or not much was wrong was happening & what are yo (u) worrying for - *looking so well* - that I - thirsty for any shadow - began to belie ve him - *wanted to* - clutching at anythi ng -

so that I fooled myself that he - the specialist - was right - meant what he was

telling her - or rather - this pleased me! - that they were wrong had got the diagnosis
all tangled up - as usual - and so I told her
this - happy & crazy & foolish - but as it turn
ed out lucky/wise - that typically they had mad
(e) a mistake - that they were wrong to have
told me that she had cancer - irreversible car-
cinoma - when in fact it was probably so
me/thing else altogether & how Sarah in
England was getting in touch w/ a special
ist & wanted us to come over etc & look
how she wasn't coughing anymore & look
ing so well as the doctor said & how we
shouldn't give up but try to find out X-
actly what was wrong & how Mary was fu
ll of the *National Geographic*'s featur
(e) on miracles(yes!) in the body's immune
system & how hers must be doing just that etc etc etc

So she knew]

& it was here - at this point - at that mo
ment - that she quietly said that she ha
(d) been 'wondering' - & *this was all she
said* - but that **this** - this one - had not oc
curred to her

# 1

As soon as she discovered what was wrong without a word to me she went to see a doctor

# 2

She & Hope [Francis] came back w/ the stark news
that the X/ray is now even worse The whole bott
om half of one lung is already gone & she has a
fever.  I've felt it in her hands for quite a while
now  -  the *'low pyreXia'*            And now the doc
confirms it

# 3

She is calm Says she feels better now she knows.
Alone here this afternoon, we wept helplessly in
each other's arms, I conscious of the fever. Said
she'll miss me had enjoyed every minute of our ti-

me together wd do it all over again if she cd but
promise her I'll carry on get married again etc

# 4

Is still like a dream She stretches out her hands
to me & smiles But alone, in repose, she's already
on her journey Please God don't make her suffer
Tell us what to do right When I got back from
Prof Wynter last night I was fooled I really crazi-
ly thought that they had made an **X**traordin
ary mistake in the reading of her condition Now
I recall Dr Morgan's 'three months' My God! That
wd be September this year or did he say six
months? Today the Prof declined making any pre
diction - still holding out Hope? - though she asked
him

# 5

[Later John and I [John LaRose, who flew in from London &
Port of Spain to be w/ us] dared SheilaW (who had done that
second X/ray for her) to give us a prognosis (though even
then I still didn't think it cd happen) which turned out ac
curate almost to the day]

# 6

**1 am**

Tonight when I came into bed, she already under
the blanket, I put my help/less arms around her &
her body was like a candle gently burning Not
her face But the body It sent a strange sensation
deep into my bowels and into my kidneys, like re-
jection And I remember now how months before I
had sensed this *alien* in her & quarrelled quarrelled quarrelled at her & realize now that it was like
I was a dog barking at some strange new presence/
some endangering intrusion

# 7

## 1: 45 am

And so she sleeps here, knowing at last of her death.  Our first night of this knowledge together

# 8

## 4 am

We woke up and could only weep in each other's
arms again, holding out against the coming light,
deep in each other's dreams

# III

# MONA

# Sunday 7 Sept 1986

Only tonight Sunday 14 December

going through my haphazard Diary again did I come

across these entries - fragments - can't even tell you

how/when I wrote them - inserted here in square

brackets - written miraculously on her birthday - on

the day she died

■

## 1

[Sad lovely Sunday, quiet here on campus at Mary's old wooden house, w/ bright sun & some wind. But it is the quiet that I love. Reminds me of Mile & Quarter days. Today is her birthday. 60 years!! No one will ever believe that! Looking so much like 40! Now lying here almost completely ruined. When I wished her Happy Birthday this morning, something like the light after a cloud on water came upon her face. Surprise? Recognition? Wonder? [Did she know that she wd die this day???] Have not been able [strong enough] to give her the gifts I'd hidden

away for her: a silver bracelet & some cloth from Sen-
egal, a watch & chocolate Geneva

Was playing our Ghana tape w/ her **X**traordinary
reading of 'Charity' (I Corinthians 13) & Lorca's 'Death of a Bullfighter' both of which I had record-
ed in Ghana w/ (on the Lorca) her reading interweav
ing w/ Miles Davis' *Concierto de Aranjuez* from **Sket**
**ches of Spain**, as if she, somehow, had created them
all into a single breathing

All this time, from dawn to about 9 am, she was
talking in her sleep, wandering & quite incoherent
Sometimes her lips moved quickly, like someone praying [This was to be repeated near midnight that night
as she approached the end] Sometimes there was a frown She was worrying about things: files, Savacou,
Michael, did we eat etc etc etc]

Then about 9:30, w/ me & Michael in the room, she
suddenly like woke up to go to the bathroom And
wondered what was wrong w/ her foot [swollen & pain

60

ful w/ the rhabdomyosarcoma]. Purple dye [like mercu-
rochrome] had been painted on it yesterday even
ing/afternoon by the nurse, Miss Mac, before she
went home

About 2 weeks ago Mary came up to Irish Town to fetch
me because a similar incident had occurred - complete
blackout of the illness & wonder at where she was/what
is she doing here etc. I suppose miracles take place like th
is - from this kind of moment - but we who love look on w/
out [sufficient] faith & understanding & so the hope gets less
the dream gets tarnished & heaven weaker weaker weaker

Michael & I had to persuade her to use the potty
next to the bed (she wanted to go to the bathroom) &
she sat down w/ her elbow on the bad foot in that
contemplative slightly straining way I know/ some
times twisting the front of her hair round a finger
as if she was okay at home . . .

When she was finished - it was water water water
water - almost black when I looked at it - & seem-

ed it wd never end (she couldn't even wipe herself proper
ly) - she wanted to stand up straight & we tried
to let her/help her but she collapsed forward into
my arms so heavy so heavy so heavy & i so help
less & happy happy happy to have her here in
my arms & I cd hold her for ever & ever & ever &
ever & she said she was sorry for the inconvenien-
ce she was putting us to & said that this was wh
(y) she wanted to be in her own house [we were to
go to 46 College Common on Monday] & why she'd ev-
en prefer to be in hospital (!) - she who so disliked
them & said she'd never go back there - the only
time in all her life w/ me I'd ever heard her tetchy/
and of course sometimes she talked/'complained' a-
bout the pain . . . [and she had to keep wetting her lips w/ her tongue all the time, I remember, and like chaw
ing her mouth because it was so dry . . . ]


**2**

Miss Mac [the 'practical nurse' - i.e. an 'untrained' 'non professional' woman skilled in 'looking after' people who are v sick or dying] arrived about 11 am & has taken over When she complained of feeling sick, Miss Mac replied **Nonsense! Look up! Open your eye & look at me.** Again this is the secret of the miracle - to com pletely believe that what's so is not so But this morning seeing her ramble like that [effect of all those pain-killing dr ugs, they said] - after such a good day yesterday - a good sleeping day, that is - no visitors - I begin to doubt [to despair of] the miracle & in fact succumbed to [what I was calling] **the Culture of Death** by asking Mary to read some 'Religious Philosophy' (Words for the Day) to her; & I played my **Poems** tape which is full of death & requie quiem music -

[Mary & Velma have been doing this anyway/ reading to her/ though I wasn't happy w/ it & said so/ which is why V eventually told me, under Mary's cherry tree, still red among green, I will always remember - [that cherry was destroyed, as was our IT 'Dump' - along w/ so much else in Ja - during Gilbert Hurricane 1988] that I w/

my 'Hope' & 'Miracle' was

# standing in the way of my wife's death!

in the way, that is, of her proper & necessary pre-
paration for it/ which is kinda strange since better than **anybody else** 'involved', Mexican, as soon as she
knew, had prepared & was preparing herself (+me!) for 'it';
don't think she really needed anybody to do 'that' for
her, though the warm & love w/ which she was surround-
ed was wonderful & helped/ helped me too - which doesn't
mean to say that we didn't have Hope. If not what wd
there be? She knew it, she feared it, she was frightened
& puzzled, I think, by it, she certainly didn't **wish** it,
but she **faced** it - in a way that I know that I cd never
do - perhaps will **never** do


None of the Friends xcept perhaps the one who carried
the name Hope (isn't that something?) seems to have understood this & judging from their behaviour after her death

seemed really to care; and I began to realize this when we had to go to Town to Campus to Mary's because she couldn't take the hills anymore or the stairs at the 'Dump' & we wanted to be nearer a doctor etc etc etc & so we thought of setting up our own place on Campus. We finally got - too late - 46 College Common - right opp 36 where we had spent so many happy years before

but it's not really so much that they don't/didn't care, as that they (we) didn't/don't understand our place & role in these moments. I mean we (they) are quite happy & sincere in coming around to look for the dead & dying - esp when female like themselves - the 'bonding' etc - (hardly any males came to see her in the time she was known to be ✖) One night I came in & found two good friends there w/ Mexican, Mexican propped up on pillows watching tv - I mean they watching & she suffering but the whole thing tryin to be 'normal' & they sincerely come to keep her 'company' & there were many more things like that

What I am saying here is that our much vaunted cultu re - culture of the people, culture of the poor, culture

of those who have suffered, negritude, the 'unspoiled so
uls', Sun People, the Wretched of the Earth etc etc etc -
just didn't seem right then & there to be 'there' when I
needed it - just didn't seem able to provide anything more
than pillow support for Mexican - & didn't - cdn't - offer me anything at all since the 'culture' has problems
w/ its males

*Of course I was trying to stand in the way of my wife'
(s) death* - wouldn't you?. But what VP didn't realize at
the time was that I was also preparing Mexican & myself for it or rather preparing ourselves as twin & couple,
*against* it & that not only did Mexican need help in all
this but perhaps even me more so - the marginal - the
marginalized - because male - survivor. Is here - to us
- that the culture has nothing to say It may need us
in bed or behind the wheel or a desk or a gun; but it
just doan know how to treat us or even 'let' & 'allow' us
when it comes to Life & Love & Food & Birth & Death &
Resurrection - though this is changing - and (we males) don't
seem to have done much about it neither . . .

some say that in these circumstances we (cripple widowers) don't
know how to ask don't know how to ask for help - but I asked & asked & asked & asked - CRIED OUT in fact & wrote it all
out not only here but in a 'published' document called **HE
LP** - but it didn't seem to make any difference - only seemed
to make people **VEX**]

Michael is cleaning the cars - is he really going
back Tuesday?. Beverley is in the kitchen. Sean is
vaguely around. Mary & Aunt May are at church
& we've been mercifully spared visitors - so far (11:30
am)

# 3
# Almost Noon

The life of this thing is so weird. When I wrote the
last entry w/ Miss Mac coming in, I was again pr-
etty optimistic/mad But Sheila's visit - her usual
warning words to me - she's going - the energy is
palpably draining away. Prepare yr/self for the

**irreversible reality & shock** /and even then I was

n't listening - I couldn't/... soon set me down again

Earlier (last week) she had given us two weeks. One
week has now gone. She's about right, I should
think. As she said, we can hope, & hope that so-
mewhere along the line there will be [may be] a br-
eakthrough - but there seldom is. There ?never is.
No miracles, Brathwaite. And I know it. She can't
even find her own mouth now - but I still hope
- [and didn't/couldn't think that when I left her that e-
vening to go back up to Irish Tn] -

# 4

[When Sheila stripped her down to sponge her &
xamine her .  her naked body stretched there on
the bed was as beautiful & as desirable as ever .
i cd have made love to her that Sunday morning
felt that accustomed leap of love the golden warm

& copper colour skin the plump & curves that I
have so long known & loved my darling Mexican]

## 5
**2:30 pm**

Sitting down to lunch on her birthday: Mary's
table [seems strangely] fiXed: glasses, plates, white starched tablecloth - six places - [Mary perhaps
also bravely carrying on as if nothing had happened!
that Death shd have no place at this Birthday
Table] - I sudden realize what a  stranger have I
become/ how I am so suddenly bereft of family

[& somehow it was that table, thoughtful & innocent &
caring, I suppose - & the tablecloth - that did it - mock
ing me somehow . . .]

Michael has gone up to IT to see about the fridge
. . . He's just-just married (we didn't even know!) liv-

ing in the States now Almost couldn't get back here (some
Immigration Problem) making his own way . . .

                                    . . . I sit out
here alone on the veranda watching silence . . .

                            . . . poor darlin
lies in her coma in the next room as if we are not
here . . .

# 6

[It is such a beautiful day: one of these drowsily
quiet Sundays, windy & cool for this time of year,
w/ that faint smell of the sea in the air as it gets
up sometimes into these valleys. No sound of an
engine, not even a bird calling . only if I listen,
the quiet surf of the leaves as if somebody is wishing through high grass If I was 12 & down in
Mile & Quarter I wd be sleeping soundly by now.
Through the latticework here on Mary's veranda I

can see the Dallas hills clear clear & hard against the sky and if I get up, I can see the little white cloud that is our house up there in Irish Tn. But is amazing how far Nature has retreated in these months since May Xcept for the incessant rains I mean you look up at the daylight moon w/ some surpri se it's there! & how Time too has been like standing still as if I fighting each day with her/for her, wr- estling out of it each precious drop & minute & ea ch morning that she still here with *yes* her smile & reassure is like starting the century all over a- gain. Only is like hammers going **WHY WHY WHY** in every corner of the green in every corner of the blue and I am always on the verge of restless an- swers which I feel somehow will bring relief & ma- ke me somehow HAPPY & so I try to concentrate on that. I mean I know they say I'll have to reconstr uct my life. Will have to. But how! and why! And will I really **have** to? And when I get to this I so me how smile that everything will be OK - that's why I wouldn't 'have to'! And everytime I get to

71

this I go back in & sit w/ her & praise the Lord th
at she still here]


[esp since I was so increasingly satisfied & in love
w/ her & what she was making with & for us And
she was so perfect w/ me I mean us two together
We were incessantly pleasantly arguing always
sharing everything even the little/est thing I saw
or heard or thought or read I'd come to her with
it & she to me Was like we danced together/ very
very well/ and at the same time gave me space/
gave me up space, which sometimes we both knew
I don't deserve/ male cheater if you can call it th-
at/ which is what I suppose some of the Woman Fr
iends (though it wasn't dem business) didnt like cdnt
stand Here is where I suspect they said she was li
ke a fool & spoiling me but she was far far far
from that . . . ]


For it was she who handled the French & Spanish
& all the hazards of all the foreign travel Who
navigated the car across Europe & into New York

& Chicago & Edinburgh & from Massachusetts to
the Miami shoreline & sometimes took over the wh
eel after midnight on those long crazy drives back from Accra on Nkrumah's new lonely highways
when possessed by the red firefly eyes of *sasabon-
sam* I was dreaming the Min$\chi$ up a tree or over th
(e) black redge of ravines . . . dealt w/ people . . .
from marketwomen to workmen to editors professor
(s) madpeople & specialists . . . Whatever else may
be fall me now after 26 years can only be cola or
coda/appendices - can only be luck/ if a lucky/ if
a don't get ill/ if a don't meet mi dessert or deserts
w/ an asp or an adder or a boa-constrictor or gor-
gon O poor little helpless What will happen to Savacou & the computers Who will love you so total
ly, friend


# 7

## After Lunch

Now, after lunch, I sit in the room w/ her. We are alone. The visitors, sensing what is happening - that she can no longer cope - have stopped coming - [or have λhausted their concern & are now waitin gatherin their sympathies for the Big Event] - tho the Irish Towners (some of them) who only now know - [during all this time I told no one/ or hardly anyone - as if it was not happening!] - or have only just been told of her true & very grave condition - may come down to see her later today . . .

[as they did five of them in Mr Hardy's blue beat-up car about 5 o'clock her last visitors ever & she opened her eyes & her mind & she smiled & talked w/ them of th emselves & old times as if nothing had happened & when they came out they ma rvelled & said Mrs B isn't as sick as they had heard had feared as they'd been led to believe . . . and went away happy/reliev ed . . . or so it seemed . . . remember?]

# 8

She lies, 'asleep', as she has been for about one week now - ever since the Irish Tn effort last Sunday [she me & Michael went back up to Irish Tn for the afternoon when she cd still struggle painfully to move - you couldn't say 'walk' - but she went up there & just looked around w/out much seeming connection - no comments - no sighs - no regrets - as if in a way it was not impossible that she wd return when she was better why not - but really not there - not really back home - no homecoming - not by a long long way. Mary or somebody in town said that perhaps she wanted the chance to talk w/ Michael & me - & perhaps she did - & perhaps we didn't help much - I know I continued to shy away from these 'moments' - though I don't think any such 'moment' was in her mind - it was already far too late for anything like that - she had 'closed her eyes to Irish Town' as she had said when she decided to stay down by Mary on campus & on this return trip never re ally opened them back . . .]

Yet last Sunday she cd still struggle to walk & sh
(e) cd still talk/ if she wished to make the effort.
By Monday/Tuesday we were talking of a walker
for her then of a wheelchair She sat in that wheel
chair only once - on Friday Miss Mac wheeled her
up & down the veranda & it was pitiful: Me χ like
a cripple Me χ like a helpless invalid w/ her emaci-
ated shoulders the darling head so even more beautiful again w/ the Afro cut by Sean held up so
hardly, so weak; her hands from time to time up to
her head her face her eyes as if to shade them from the sunlight through the lattice - or her mind
- poor darling - from the world . . .


## 9

Now she lies in bed, 'asleep' . . . [and I remember how
sometimes I wd come down from Irish Tn in the middle
of the night & tiptoe to her window & look in on her sleeping:
the white high pillow her head to one side ever so gent

ly the tears filling my eyes like the dark sky and I cd
see her softly breathing and it gave me hope still
always hope . . . ]


. . . dozing . . . perhaps trav

elling . . . powdered by Miss Mac so that there is
no sweat right now [so much sheer liq
uid came out of that brown
body this day] & there is the fan Mary bo
rrowed from the Chapel so that it's cool in here . . .
From time to time her voice . . . coming as from
far away . . . wandering . . . the lips moving as if
muttering or even praying & then the mouth falling open as she goes off to sleep . . . & coming on
to that beautifully sculptured my dearly beloved
('s) brow [more beautiful perhaps in suffering now] . . . a
frown . . . which from time to time I try to smooth
away . . .


■

■

How God has come to punish me not cherishing enough:
the long nights I sometimes/ too too often surely/ was a-
way/ the smell of other muses on my breath/ the tales
she must have heard the agonies of doubt/selfdoubt her
love might well have tried to justify xplain/xplain away
forgive & must have caused her generosity to hide &
harbour like a pearl inside her heart/her hurt until it
built itself into this tumour and how I feel Olorun/God
has now withdrawn from me because I did not preciate
ijs gifts of àshe: the always possibility: creative cross-
roads: open doors: Mawu Ogou the Eshu/Legba: loas



■

If she should die - go from me now - why why why
why - I know I will not only lose my life my love my love
- my very very very friend - and there are o too few of these - I
may forever lose the light the light - the open doors

Who knows
how - why - what -
even our love creates

# MEDICAL CERTIFICATE OF THE CAUSE OF DEATH

7 September 1986


Metastases to lung, brain & muscles

[thighs]


Leimyosarcoma at uterus


60 years


Sister-in-Law's Residence


3 Gibraltar Camp Road, UWI, Mona

11:55 pm

# IV

# MIDDLE PASSAGES

Sunday 7 September 1986

**1**

Tonight - at midnight [just before midnight]
Me𝒳ican died - peacefully, thank God

**I was not there**

Had gone to Irish Tn to finish **Jah Music** & her
**Bibliography** It seems that around 10 o'clock she
woke up & asked to sit in a chair. Her breathing,
which Mary had said she wasn't happy about
**even before I left** *[I heard her say it, aloud to
herself but really to me I'm sure now. If communication
between us had been better, we might have spoken more
about it - rather I might have picked up her warning
signal]* had become shallow & agitated

Mary phoned Sheila who said she was coming over & asked for oxygen Mary eventually got this
from Mrs Minott at the Nurses School. Velma
meanwhile went for Miss Mac, who w/ Michael,
was from now w/ her all the time. Kitty Beckford
[who never became a 'formerFriend' but remained a rare
& help & strength long after these events]

tried phoning me (phone responding busy as usual) up at Irish Tn. She then went back home but was too worried to remain there. She came back to Mary's w/ George & was just in time to pray with & for her

It seems that after sitting in the chair for a while/ she didn't seem comfortable/ kept trying to put her feet on the floor (as she'd tried to do that morning) Miss Mac then asked her if she wdn't be more comfortable back on the bed Michael lifted her back there (or helped her back there)

The breathing all this time continued agitated Kitty says that it was like coming from the very depths of her She asked for a glass of water Took like two spoonsfull & relaxed/ folded her hands across her chest as if in prayer

**Yes**

said Miss Mac

### Yes darling

she knew then she says she was making it
through

### Yes my love

She looked across at Michael then, for a while,
then turned back to herself, her lips moving as if
in prayer, Michael lying at the foot of the bed

**When I look at him** says Miss Mac **I cd see
he was down But he never leave her Not
a soul wd have move Michael from that
room that night**

Velma said it was Sean & Kitty & Aunt May I
suppose who went out for the oxygen

**His foot was touching her body
all the while**

Miss Mac said

## And I not there

A little more water and then she was quiet

Very very quiet/ her hands holding Miss Mac's

tightened tightened tightened then relaxed

And it was quiet in the room like that When

Sheila arrived When the now useless oxygen

arrived When Kitty came back with GBeck & they

prayed then & prepared the body & Mary lit the

candle & her body was covered with a white sheet

& Mary met me at the door with an eventual

She's gone & I went inside & saw her: all my life

all all my love & hopes & dreams & past & future

still quiet on that bed & gone in the quiet flicker-

ing light of Mary's candle & there was no sound

in all the world that Sunday midnight which

went on & on & on forever

# 2

[Up at Irish Town I must have just dotted the last i of her Bibliography (of

my work) I was typing for her . Since the New Beacon edition of it which

she had submitted & had had accepted some yrs before didn't look like it

was coming out - not at least, she said, in the near future - & laughed that

kind of brief soft wry laugh at  the 'situation' - and, she said, she had so

much wanted to see it out  - I had undertaken - promised myself  - to type

an  (updated) version of it for her for Savacou - and she still had the streng-

th to say that she wanted to say a few words of 'Introduction' - and did it -

[1 Aug 86] - just as she had gone on working at the Tourist Board Library

until she just couldn't go no more -

> [there are now two versions of her Bib:
> the Savacou version (1986) that I fin-
> ished typing on the night she died/it
> was movingly launched in October 86
> by Cliff Lashley at the Institute of Jamai
> ca, where for yrs she was a part-time
> librarian; and the memorial New Beacon
> edition which appeared in 88]

- and my working on this Bib became my life - kind of - not only because I

had promised her,  but because it was her work &  therefore her life that I

was dealing with esp since it was her life dealing with my life - if you see

what I mean - and the routine of doing it & checking it etc etc etc became

like a steadying creative creature effort for me [a loveline lifeline] & I

began to tell myself that as long as I was doing this - for her - she wdn't -

cdn't - somehow - die - [the first time I was perhaps even consciously using the
word] - & I had just I suspect dotted the last i of it that night - when she died
- w/ the computer room in darkness xcept for the old black anglepoise &
no clock in the room up there

# 3

I must have switched off the light then & must have dozed or something when
someone like a voice calling me awake woke me up w/ like a high mournful cry in
all that Irish Th midnight & dark & quiet like the white owl that had startled us
on our first night up there when we cd at last move into the what we were calling
'The Dump' & had opened the bedroom door to the back porch where I worked
most of the days after that which was open to our high green lawn up against the
mountain on one side & ran down into the deep gully that marked our boundary
on the other & this white owl must have been sitting on this huge dark passion-
fruit tree when we opened the door & came flying towards us w/ out sound just
the white flashing like the mournful cry that now wake me up w/ like Michael's
voice now somehow calling out

*'Daaaaaaaaaaaaaaaaaaaaaad eeeeeeeeeeeeeeeeeeeeeeeeeeeeeeeeeeeeeee'*

like long & mournful in the dark like that & I decided right then & there to get
back down to town as fast as possible]

90

**4**

As I went up the steps I heard Mary's coug

(h) so I knew she - they - were awake [but

half-hoped-Ҳpected to find **all** of them sitt-

ing up because MeҲ couldn't sleep or some-

thing But Mary] met me at the door [so I

must have known and so] I must have ask-

ed like this cd be the last moment of my

life - w/ the white silent hoot of the owl

going tut tut tut in my head -


**What's happening** &

she started to say **Nothing** then s

said [simply] **She's gone**

[like that and i think turned away from the

door] and i must have said **When**

- like STUPID/ in increasing cleft & shock

& silence - there are no WORDS for this


**5**

91

Miss Mac was there, walking about in the sitting/ sinking room & Aunt May was lying on the settee as if sleeping

Michael [who had been w/ her all the while/ thank God for that] had gone out, ridden by his own grief [He'd been in the room Mary says [as Miss Mac had said] curled up at the foot of the bed crying quietly. He wept all through the funeral service too & from time to time afterwards] trying to control his - [still can't find the word for this - bottomless emotion]


## 6

i went into the room, candle burning, her same face bound in death/ that white gauze round her features She was so peace, so still, so beautiful . still X pected her to open those eyes & call my name in her sleepily way when I come in late . . .

# 7

[i went in several times - kept going in & going back out again & again -

crushed & reduced like something in a fist - like something in a fist of sp-

ace i walked upon - no hard - no smooth - no earth - no Mary's wooden floor


- as if i wasn't really there - and worrying about the faint trace - something li

ke a frown i thought i saw but did not wish to see upon her dream & with a ki

nd of gusting deep inside me like a coming storm [as it still gusts/ Th Octo


ber 9 now - one month later/ time has stopped/stood still and i am still/ if

anything *collapsed/* & still there in that room with her & with that moment

& it  is as if the earth already on its curve towards the sun towards the stars &


she about to curve along its curve still as the fields but floating like them

slowly now by water but still still - not fully yet stretched fully out but wait-

ing still & silent for the tide and i am walking to/toward(s) her to that almost


stone & still the love & **person** i had known but somehow gone away  & si-

lent from me though it was as if she cd still speak & perhaps did but now so

distant/ near me/ distant that i never reach where she is floating from me on my naked feet/ i feel the clicks the stones the thorns the plimplar & the weed

(s) cutting me & catching at me as i toil & toil towards her w/out moving as

she moves/ as i move forward as she does not move & so is near & dear & dis

tant as my sister's candle & its shadows that like softly wash her face w/ ripp

le fingers/ & in my knuckle hands/ gripped in my empty fist this iron bar of

cold & guilt of being absent from this place when she was present in it/ pass-

ing from it needing/ calling out for absent me that never now & ever was her

love her lover/ too late now & foot & bottom of her bed that i now walk to-

wards & walk towards & walk towards between these leaves of shadows/ dredg-

ing towards her in this ploughed up/ unploughed field & w/ this bar i have my

hands on/ gripping gripping as i say the cold & iron of the life/ the death i

can no longer live between & can now never reach but toil towards/ her toil

towards/ her over barren fertile fields & harrowing the broken earth between

us in my mind forever cleft & cracked w/ pain - the pain that troughs within

me as i walk towards the silence i will never reach so near so near & floating

slowly from me in this slowly drifting stationary room that has become our

world that can become no other world that never can be world for us again

And is only today (15 March 92 + 15 August 92) after so much more unhapp has

happened happened happened & still a doan reach yet [see for xample Trench Tn

Rock' *Hambone* (Aug 1992)] & recognize this Middle Passage passage that a li-

mbo/lembe thru is what the **Second K'un** has said me all along like no like

n/ like yes/terday a thousand years away]


## 8

**Had brought down the adinkra cloth** [won
der what made me take it from the cupboard up at Iris
(h) Town/ Had wanted I think to fly it crazy from the
back ledge of the car as a sign & signal to the world th
at something sacred in a way was happening so it was
there in the car already] **I covered her with it** [pl
aced it over the white sheet that covered her so
carefully so carefully so very very tenderly]


## 9

**[Another entry, marked 5 am]**

95

**W**hen I went into the room the candle had burned down so that she

was now different in the bed - looked  different on the bed as if the place &

certainly the **time** had somehow shifted. All was in shadow now  She seem-

ed much further down much lower in the bed the water of the candle

shallower there was no tide no drifting now & yet she had like drifted

further much much further And yet when I lifted up the candle to see if I

cd see what/what had happened - why the change the change - and looked

again upon her face - **my Mexican was**

**smiling** and i did not know i did not know how to go to go out

slowly or to **rush** / telling Miss Mac Aunt May & Mary but they had

seen already - they all knew


## 10

**Then Mary & I went** [over to 46 College Common - th

(e) [University] house we'd got for her - we were to move

in Monday - *that's today!* ] **to phone the Undertaker**

**I spoke w/ Thels** [in London] **Mary tried John** [LaRo

se] **& George** [D's cousin/ in NY] **but cdn't get them**

## 11

### My prayer as we prayed:

[first Mary, then Miss Mac, then Aunt May, last me, in Mary's veranda in the still dark but dawn-coming-up-morning soon after they had taken her body away about 5:45 am] (i wrote this out soon after, trying to remember the words)

Mary's was formal & Christian Miss Mac's was easy & nation Aunt May's simple & direct Like the people themselves I had to wrench the words out of myself w/ none of their ease & power w/ my tear (s) like a wail or wall I had to break thru break thru break thru & I spoke slowly between deep br eaths As if it was the first time in my life I'd ever prayed - & indeed it was - first time I ever had to/ wished to/ wanted/ NEEDED to - and not for some-THING but for someONE - [and like it didn't matter if the form was **Christian** or **Islam** or **Rasta** or **Pagan** or **Vodoun** - and the words didn't much matter neither -

[in fact looking at them now they look trivial - I mean like 'no big ting' - but the weight of their meaning was heavy - like stones that morning - it felt heavy & slow - heavy & slow - like that - coming out of me unrolled away from deep deep down & dungeon]

## 12

Lord we thank you . . .

for this life . . .

for D's beauty & courage & understanding . . .

She brought all this . . . into my life . . .

and I know . . . she brought it too to those who . . .

came to . . . know . . . and . . . love her . . .


Thanks too for the love & support of my sister &

Aunt May who came all the way from Barbados to

help us . . . and for allowing Michael to be here . . . to

let him know how much we bless him . . .

love him cyaaan done . . .

**and for Miss Mac . . . who in these last few critical days**

**. . . brought . . . such strength and solace . . . not only**

**to . . .** [i could not call the name] **. . . but to me -**

**and all of us here in this house**

[What I will always love about

Miss Mac is the way, from the ve-

ry first greeting, she took to Meχ-

ican (& she to her/ she trusted her

w/ all that pain - or rather - trust-

ed unto her & even **into** her - that

pain) - the complete contact of her

body w/ her body - the houmfort

& confidence engendered - and the

sense of faith. Miss Mac brought

warm black sunlight into Meχ's he-

art & hoom - I know that - and it

helped & settled us. No well-paid

primpy nurse in uniform has this -

does this - can offer this - like salt

- like charcoal - sunlight - h/earth - the human heal. And I thank

God I can now pray w/ her


And Aunt May?  Collector of coral

& beautiful sea-stones/ you came

from Bajan w/ yr 80 years that I

wd never guess you carried/always

so young in voice in body all my

life that I have - ah - that I have

taken like for granted. You stayed

w/ us & stood w/ us at Irish Tn &

then at Mary 's up at all hours all

night long like when I found you

sleeping ℷhausted on the redrose

couch the night she died - the old

er generation of our family - you,

Aunt Eleanor  Aunt Edith, our Mo-

ther & our Father/ helping us  frai

ler so-called younger ones along th

(e) way & asked us nothing /ask-

ed for nothing simply brought yr

smile yr commonsense yr love yr al

ways i-tal/natural & I thank God

tonight that I can pray w/you]

I thank you for the life she lived . . .

that you . . . gave her . . . that she . . . gave us . . .

and may she rest in peace

And we all said Amen then

— —

## 13

And as the dawn was coming up coming up coming up making it deeper & deeper & darker they
came in Sam Isaac's hearse & took her away in th
(e) white winding sheet her whole self wrapped a-
way and I too wrapped/ wrapping my own sheet ti
ghter & tighter round my/self/ my body/ like for co
mfort & for strength/to stand up to stand up at
all/ to keep myself in & from like flowing out or fo
llowing away as if I should be going too - w/ her

- where ever she was going - and it was if I knew
or rather felt she wasnt sure (I wasn't sure)/ she cdn't
see (I couldnt see)/ & this white sheet was comfort -
let me tell you/ I squeezing it tighter tighter roun
(d) me as i following like helplessly like helplessly this soft dark horse/ looking like any ordinary
car or horse or hearse - but larger - longer - lean-
er - and so very very very different - so quietly
quietly special w/ not a sound of wheels along th
(e) russet-leaf-stained-almond-curve of the road fr
om Mary's house behind me where they had kind-
ly left me to this cruel mercy by my onesome - on
ly this gentle rise & foil as if they being careful
down the now cold steps past perfume tree &
cherry tree & the almonds & the jacaranda bush
the broken little white Gibraltar Camp gate & then
the darker darker river of the road away from me
from me from me from me & the chill & silent &
still darkness of that foreday morning & then nothing nothing nothing nothing nothing I cd do cd
do cd ever do again w/ her for her for her for her
for her as they ride away in the grey & the dark

& the silence & the sky above me one alone here
now like the now really lonely morning star more
lonely w/ the soft & faintest pin & pink of wind on
all those other softly fading stars that somehow
reach & touch & reach & touch the silver of my
face

# Letter to Zea
# Mexican

### Sunday 14 Sept 1986 2am

# Dearest Mexican

Tomorrow afternoon I'll see yr face for the last time see you for the
last last time I really can't imagine that, you know

From the very first I saw you I
**knew** . I was certain . And I have always been secure w/ you.
Standing near to you at Mother's
funeral when I didn't know how I
wd survive & might have tumbled
into her grave - at least that's how
I felt - or when my head was spin-
ning in that bathroom in the vill-
age near Cambridge or in our bedroom up in Irish Tn & I shouted
out & you come running & hold
me & tell me not to worry & it wd
pass Or when it felt like fainting
at Worcester on the way to G K
Hall of all places! or in that mid-

day in the middle of Delhi & again you told me **I cd do it**. You
always said that & I believed you
because I believed in you . I trust
ed you & I knew you cd be trusted
What a wonderful thing . I realize
now I always knew that nothing
cd come between us I  knew for in
stance that if a gunman came into
the house we wd prob die together
die for each other I certainly knew
that I wd die for you if/when I had
to & you I'm even surer wd have
died for me too as you almost did
once as it is though now I'll never
be able to prove that or anything
else for that matter but what a world when you have to even **think**
you have to!

Seems such a short time we were
together In fact feels like no time

at all **Contracted to a**

**Span** Mary says but let's hope

that it'll lengthen back out. Every

one has been wonderful supportive

etc [little **did I know that this**

**wd not continue**] though of cour

se I continue to be like dark like

doubt like down/ shut dumb & can

not be consoled **How cd I ever be!**

Each day I came to love you more

appreciate you more & more So th

at Sarah cd write that even though

she didn't see so much of you in

London in recent years I always br

ought yr **presence** w/ me And as

I've told you several times during

& after Worcester & the **comput-**

**ers**, there was - cd be - no one

**else** no matter what you or any-

bodyelse might think or say This

was the golden time/ finding as I

said our own lifestyle at/in IT-Pen

lyne-Bdos & the the trips abroad
& Velma painting lovely word-pic
tures - **and how greedily I believed them & why not** - of you &
me at IT growing old like once up
on a time & doddery but everlast-
inglovingly together


George is here & is ecstatic about
the house & full of ideas for im-
provement Seems so strange & such a pity we never invited him ov
er even for a brief weekend /to wh
ich I hear you say But doan mine
George! I always askin when he
comin & he always busy-busy-bu-
sy/ & he confirm this sayin how
you always askin & how he alway
(s) fine he busy busy busy/ But
now he's here one wishes it cd have been the two of you laughin &
talkin loud & happy & trampin up

& down the place - you w/ yr off-
white jippi-jappa on lookin at wh
ere 'the road' wd be etc Am sorry
too we never phone Aunt Eleanor
at least from time to time/ kept
more in touch w/ them altho again
I hear you laugh that how Ant Ell-
en too confuse man & of course th
ere wd be time another time etc
etc etc But the phone was loud &
clear when I got through to New
Amsterdam to Uncle Time as it tur
ned out & after shock & disbelief
he seemed to take it cool although
I know it lick him down but said
it was a good thing *he* pick up the
phone because if it was Eleanor it
surely wd have kill her & I ask
George to phone again today to
find out how they are/ she take a
'turn' he say & now her eyes are
red & fat w/ weeping . . .

And you, my love? Can
you see me? Hear me?
Are you close by? Ang-
ry? Frustrated? Reliev-
ed? Delighted? Amused?
Sorry? Puzzled? Lonely?
Far away? Desolate? In-
different? Different? The
same? Changing? And if
so how? Do I affect you?
Do you affect me? Are
you okay? Are you ha-
ppy or still suffering?
What is it like & how is
it w/ you across the wa-
ter/ or is there nothing
nothing nothing at all
as I think you xpected
as I think you sometime
(s) said tho I not too too
sure bout that At least

you always said you tr-
ied to be philosophical
about death & dying .
but from the poems you
loved & cd quote about
the cosmos & from the
way you kneeled at chu
rch & prayed etc etc I
know you felt that there
was something more so-
mething much much mor
(e) to make it all worth-
while & you were very
strong on 'retribution' (y-
ou felt at least it ought to 'hap
pen') & wondered why it
seems the good get oft-
en nothing

Miss Mac has turned all the beds

out & yr chairs over up at Irish T

so that you won't able to come ba

ck to harm us!! Isn't that odd? Wh

en of course I **want you back** .

Need you back . Here w/ me w/ us

But dem seh that yu diffrent now .

As if you cross some Great Divide

or Water and are now some some-

thing Dangerous & Other . some

something Different & Alien & e-

ven it seems Ugly . Can you imag

ine how this makes me feel? Mary

speaks about

# The
# Cloud
# of

# Wit-
# ness-
# es.

whatever that is that further fright-

ens dis/stresses me Suppose dem

don't even want you to **Go & Be**

**a Beneficent Spirit & Come**

**to us in the Morning** as I

say in the poem - one of yr favouri-

tes - you asked me to read for you

from **Islands** & which Mary read

at yr Thanksgiving/ & the Congo

Square Writers - Tom Dent & dem

in New Orleans - sent a loving ca-

ble quoting from **Mother Poem**

# -She
# is
# alpha
# is
# omega
# she is
# happ
# y -

I hope so, love. You **deserve** it,

if I may put it that way. You deser

ve the best the best the best there

is mek I tell you And all the letters that have come have joined  in

this growing chorus


## Doris was gold Do ris is gold from Ramases

of all people but I bless him for it

for is true - in **all** yr names, rem-

ember?


And yet I have 'blasphemed' again

st you - because I love you so so

utterly/securely like John Figueroa

saying once how good Catholics

cd afford to criticize their Church

because they loved it so & it was

big & strong enough to clude th-

em in its faith & even in their cur

ses So that you gave me the ener-

gy even to be 'unfaithful' though I

was never that/ sharing the munifi

cence you gave w/ others though

it was that/not that/ but it must ha

ve hurt/ you always said you cdnt

understand . What worries me *(is*

*too late now)* is that I don't kn

ow how & how far deeply down it

really hit you hit you hurt you - &

if it cause the cancer


**And me? In the first pl-**

**ace I can't imagine life &**

**love w/ out you. Can't see**

**how I'll manage either .**

**Lovers muses girl-frenns**

**helpers will never be en-**

**ough & I have to be a-**

**ware/beware of frittering**

**the energy . of getting**

**too involved in things I**

**won't be able to get out**

**of - as you have warned**

**me many many times -**

dangers & **voiolen**
**ce** as a result of such

entanglements of my ow

(n) luck of what my Mo-

ther once called **cir-**
**cumspection**

& no you now to stand

beside me stand up in fa

ct in front of me to co-

mfort & forgive me


*Now you have gone*
*into that light of*
*which you were al-*
*ways a part Every-*
*one speaks of yr ra-*
*d i a n c e* **T his**
**man    proud**
**of you Mex**
**ican** *As I was fro*
*(m) the very beginn-*
*ing when you first*

walked towards me
at Norm's party &
KP noticed . . . but
never more so than
the day I took you
home to Round Hou
se & Mile & Quar-
ter & everyone
from Mother to
Mudds & Joan &
Aunt Edith & Aunt
May & Daddy O'
Neale & St Elmo to
Richard & Myrtle
& Francina & Un
cle Carlyle & Cyrille
& Uncle Lawson &
Victoria & KP's mo
ther Mama Pile co-
mes to me as if in
shock &

yes yes yes
yes yes yes
yes
She is the
one is the
one is the
wonderful/
my lady of
the gold of
the gold of
the golden
warakuna
skin: my tê
my tê my

Tete-
mexti-
canl

VI

# ΑΨΑΜΑ'Σ
## ΛΕΤΤΕΡ

Monday Mins After 5 / 15 September
**Outside Mona Chapel**

**Today is the day. When they Lay her to rest. And may her soul Rest in PEACE. For she Completed a cycle .**

[But she did not, my love. The circle knew its curve, was coming ro und w/ verve & confidence & the 'completion' was it seemed another thirty years away. The tragedy for me & if you will allow what some people will call 'arrogance' - *what right have you to arrogate such high importance to yr work?* - is that I was on the verge - indeed into a new pathway - of new work - I cd **feel** it going well/thi ngs happening This 1986 alone **Savacou** published four titles &

I wrote & revisited $\chi$/**Self** put together my Early Poems and an Index of them (but no publisher!), finished (but never forwarded!) the Great River Valley Rebellion mono graph for Barry Higman, edited th (e) Tony Bland poems for **Savac- ou** (we got it out the day he died/so he never saw what he wanted to so much); there was the pub in Belgium (Leuven/Liège) of **The visibility trigger** w/ Fr trans by Christine Pagnoulle (**Le détonateur de visib ilité**) won the Casa Prize for **Root**

(s) - not to mention the Penlyne
Coffee Operation now practically fallen into the sere into the dry rot/
Her own wonderful work at the To
urist Board Library & the offers
coming in from other Special Lib-
raries +of course my 24-mile-an-
hour day at Mona (how long will I be
able esp now Aya, to keep on teaching
all-time like this & still keep on w/
the poems of the other life which is
really the same life & the whole life
the real life /but not allowed so by ho
(w) people here see things/ As you kn

ow we went up to IT to create like a Ma
roon community/independent & subsist-
ent likethat/with enough land & space
& shall we say SPIRIT POWER for people to work/to 'find'/ develop ourselves & from/to where I cd eventually re-
sign from the University [HOW GOD DIS-
POSES, eh?] & devote all/the rest of my
blk puddin & souse to that worldpool
of writing etc since I find that it takes
more & more time & more & more ener
gy & more & more LOVE

so that it hurt when people don't seem
to understand this, the grapple w/ the
loa, they seeing the writing as a 'hobby'/**my 'hobby'** as one of our Vice-
Chancellors once told me! & call me
un-/or anti-/social because as things
stann now I find I must *defend* the wh
at-happens-when-we-say-writing - th
at kind of 'catness' in a way - when o-
thers are out visiting or laughing or
drinking or debunking or partying or
just ST/ing - which is what I'd like to
be doin too- why not! - but you can't
do everything, since this loving in the
spirit', as you put it, comes first first
first/ the thousand hour days or years
you have to spend upon the pound or
poem of the flesh to make it into LIG
HT)

130

& all this time Death there aroun
(d) the corner, in the shadows, sit
ing down w/ us at supper or our
birthday dinner, slipping in our
very cup So that me can't even s p
e ak Aya of **cycle completed** o n
ly of circle mash up & circle destroyed in the very middle of our
fortune]


**. . . coming on earth in a
physical form from her mother's womb on 7 September
and leaving 7 September It
is often [only] after physical
death that we appreciate a
one more For while she suff
ered you suffered And her
pain was your pain**


[But my pain continues, Aya, for
the very reason that I just tellin
you A circle has been broken & I
& what was once the friends &
people of the cycle/circle have so
disintegrated/ centre gone/things
fall a/part/ things fall a/part I
know there is some ritual I've not
performed/ which I don't even kn
ow/ & no one that I know/knows
how to bring it/ help me/ with it
to/wards it Which the Africans
know Which the Greeks knew It's

131

there in **Odale** & in Eliot's **Cock
tail Party** & at the end of **O l e
Story Time** But is missing in
me/with me, Myaya. I have not ev-
en **seen** her yet She has not even
**dreamed** me yet Has sent no whis
per of a message - bird or butter-
fly or curse - not even rat-bat owl
or johncrow/**Why is dat?**]

**Just could not resist listening to Rex** [Nett-
leford/reading his Tribute] **W ould not feel justifi-
ed without peeping inside.** [Did you see that large warm congregation, Aya? so many many comfort faces like Ma
ry's 'Cloud of Witnesses'? & the high banks of glowing flowers/
surprising me into a strange & unexpected strength from like a-
ll the world & then I cd not break up/break down/ but stand
up/stand up/ look around at all this love for her] **Trying to
make out who was Michael. Was he sitt
ing to your right?**

**[But] words are not working right now.
Did not come inside With the general
gathering, Kamau, sat out here and shared with you. The preacher** [Philip Potter]
**is preaching now. He is finish now. Silen**

132

ce. Who is coming neXt? A woman's [Mary's] voice Sounds like a prayer [reading from Islands]

So on this ground
write
within the sound
of this white limestone vèvè
talk
of the empty roads
vessels of your head
claypots shards ruins

And, right now, I wonder how Doris would have liked this evening to have been. How close to her ideal it went. How contented she left us. How rested her soul . . . right now. And how she must respect Kamau for his firmness and his input into the proceedings. And wonder if she would not have preferred his total organizing of events. Although he did much . And wonder about her

**reflections before she went last Sun day, in the few moments of Coherence. A strong voice . . .**

[George Watts her cousin (like-her-brother) flew in from New York. Her only relative present. Her Mother died in 72/ same year as **Mother Poem** & (dedicated to her along w/ my own Mother) & Aunt Eleanor in New Amsterdam/Berbice, the last rock of her **nam,** not well enough to travel so far so suddenly so soon. George & his wife Eileen (now divorced) were the first family of hers I met when I went to Gtown in 1960 'for her'; stayed in their wooden harp of a Georgetown hoom where she too lived George's voice (he was a motorcycle cop back then & sang in the famous Guyana Police Force Male Voice Choir) was always strong ... Was good/was very glad he came ... he spoke]

**. . . of Doris' life now. And every word can be heard from here . . .**

And on this sailing ground
sprinkled with rum, bitten
with the tenor of your open wound

walk

134

walk

the hooves will come, welcomed
by drumbeats into your ridden head
and the horse, cheval of the dead

charade of la mort

tongued with the wind
possession of the fire
possession of the dust

sundered from your bone
plundered from my breast
by ice by chain by sword by the east wind

surrenders up to you the graven Word
carved from Olodumare
from Ogun of Alare from Ogun of Onire
from Shango broom of thunder and Damballa
Grand Chemin


**And now, give thanks for having shared
. . . chants being played now, and all
rise. You looking so sweet and honest
and genuine, through the window. Not ut
tering a word and hardly knowing when
the singing will start again and when to
sit down. Lengthy singing follows. You
went around and said something in some-**

one's ear [to ChoCho Dawes who wd sing the Damirifa]

**And all the time keeping that blackness.**

**And looking so regal in that black . . .**

Looks like you are leaving now. An African song being sung [the Damirifa]. And the richness of this evening climaxes here. Or maybe you just sat down. The choir going further up. Looks like they're preparing to depart. A car starting up. And, as the service ends, my taut efforts to contain these tears also ends, and they are released. The hearse passes down towards the gate

[And do you know, Aya, that I didn't see it? didn't see it leave? didn't know when it left? I had come out with the coffin & the bearers etc and was standing near but then people started to surround me come up to me say things say things & before I knew it I was alone & it was dark & she was gone. Praise Jah that you were there to see her leave this place for me Praise Jah, Myaya, you was there my eyes her eyes our ears although I never see you . . . ]

I hope people told Doris what is being apostroph-
ised now. Sincerely hope so. And, I hope they
did when she was where, in her life She could di-
gest it. And I know you did, Kamau. For you
would not be Kamau if you did not. And I hope
they don't mess up, too much what she did. For
it is impossible to expect them not to do even a
little messing up . . .

# [And after this she adds her Blessing]

Add I hope Caribbean Arts [the Caribbean Artists Movement & no doubt the movement towards Caribbean Arts gener-
ally] and the library at Tourist Board and the Irish
Tn Citizens Association, and what more there might
have been, will grow from strength to strength. And
SAVACOU too

[But how? how Aya? How? I know
we never know these things Inscr-
utable Future etc But might it not
be that this is an end/the end rather than the continuation we ho-

pe it might be? the new beginning
we hoped it should be? like the tu
lip tree now thankfully green &
growing? but for me the opposite
the cycle now unable to re/spin?]

**Even now, she must appreciate your idea to cremate
her** [Not mine, my love Not mine But hers Always was hers/ that poem
'Charity'/ the *body to be burned* ] **and to keep the crowd at a
distance. 'Cremation at a later date'. That just fixed
it. And them.**

**What must Michael be saying? What must be his
thoughts? What must your communication be like.
And tonite, as you both go home, as you both Left
to your peace and your quietness, then what must
you think? What must you both do, as the two
Who must have meant the most to her. And What
must she think of you both now. How often will
she speak to you both, as she no doubt perpetu-
ally protects you.**

**Kamau might write to her. Kamau might think and
not transfer them to paper. For, to have as your**

man a BLACK ICON is reason for such a conscious honest woman to guard him and his
seed

The lights are out in the chapel now. The Lull re
turning. And, I must want him to have moments
to himself; but must plea his forgiveness if I helplessly share them with him. For, I am with you
Kamau. And feel even richer in the quiet commun
ication. And give thanks for you. And give thanks to Jah for your creation. And give thanks to
your Parents for you And give thanks to [Mexi-
can] for preserving the inner You. But words, Kamau, words are not enough . . .

for on this
ground

trampled with the
bull's swathe of
whips
where the slave at
the cross-roads
was a red anthill
eaten by
moonbeams by the
holy ghosts
of his wounds

the Word becomes
again a god

and walks
among us —

look —
here are his
rags

here is his crutch
and his satchel
of dreams

here is his hoe and
his rude implements

on this ground
on this broken
ground

# VII

# 'The working muses nourish Hector/Hero of Time'

Wilson Harris/ **Eternity to Season**

**I**t was AJS, [then over 70 & himself married to Elma for 45 yrs] who best, as poet to poet, spoke to me about the meaning of the loss of the poet's wife & the threat this loss is to the poetry - my now *widowered* im

ages! AJ said in his letter of condolence (& these have

all been so rich so warm so healing)


## 16 Sept 1986

. . . As I experience it, it is the nature of the poet

to base a great deal of his self, poise & creativity,

on his oneness with his wife & the happiness of

shared memories . . .


&

Bob Stewart

sent this poem


> She was the ring
> that moored your
> love and now
>
> this small circle
> falls broken
> from your hand.
>
> The wider or-
> bits of your
> life stagger

to regain
their sun-
dered centre.

The turn of memory
will find an axis
in your heart

Remembering
Doris

and  sending  you  peace

and  love  -

20  Sept  1986


&

Sunitha Kathyra Byrappa (17 Sept 1986) who not so

long before had sent me the most beautiful tribute I have

read about our Mother along, that is, w/ Christine [Craig]'s 'Round

House' Poem


I envied her being your wife and
had even expressed how nice it
was [must be] to be addressed as
Doris Brathwaite! . . . She was
part and parcel
of everything you did . . .

147

[&

Odale II *claimed over the telephone from New York:

But Kamau! She was you right hann, mann!'

And then was silent . . .]


. . .


she shared your world
so understandingly
in a compassionate way.
She could be strict with you in
a tender way - this is what I
observed in her when you both
were together. She was a person
who knew where to pull your
strings, stop at the right
moment, warn you, advice you
and inspire you. She never
allowed you to go astray [true]
She was your emblem of love
Who will there be to share [yr
poems] with/

# who will there be to write them for?

**W**hich brings me to the **CREATIVE EKB** the poet, okay? And the

now (I feel) **unprotected sources of the poetry:** the hinterland of symbol tuned

& turned to salt Which shd have been my FIRST point, since this is really

where it all begins & ends. That I did not, felt I cd not, place it first &

**foremost** (as it shd be) is the CROSS & CRUX of the PROBLEM Has

always been. People, I fear (& that inc my own family) prefer to see me,

sign me in, as **lecture, professor, History, University, Academie,**

okay? But **Kamau? poet?** What a way things begin to get  dicey &

apologetic in this area! As if, as Derek Walcott put it some time ago, a

(nigger) poet is twice the world's joke. As if you have no right to writing.

Indeed one 'formerFriend' said (**X**plained/**X**pained) as I spoke to her of

her (really 'their') **neglect,** that I am being  **punished** (her choice of word!)

because I'd gone to live 'up in' Irish Tn **pretending to be a poet** (again,

I shame to say, those are the words)


And even Mex & Mother, although they tried the **K**, cdn't really manage

it, though Mother didn't do too bad . considering . . . And like Phi the night

before the Chapel Service talkin about *how he wd begin his sermon with*

*'Eddie' & I asked why not Kamau & he replied that it was the general*

# 𝒸𝑜𝓃𝓈𝑒𝓃𝓈𝓊𝓈

(again - his word!)

that on this occasion . . . (too scared too sacred for Kamau?) & how I am

universally(!) known as E . . .


to which to my delight [my sister] Thels

pipes up w/ **But he's also 'universally' known as K**

she actually said **Kamoo** like **Kow** - you know - as most

Barabajans do but at least she tried to defend her brother

& Philip in the end 'relented' in his sermon w/ **Eddie &**

then **Eddie Kamau** though never once **Kamau**


but Philip glad to say, got over all this long ago & he & Bärbel have become good

newfriends in many many subtile ways]

150

But this willful definition of the I against the xpress wishes of the I/ this
downing of the art & writer is like part & as dem seh parcel of a-we Culture -as-antiCulture - the 'battle' of&for Identity - of Rule & Rôle in dis-ya
Caribbean 'basin' . . .

And as long as that is so, the poet can live only underground or marginal
i.e when & only how the Others want him to And comes up/ comes out/
only for the while he wins a prize(?) does a successful(?) reading or has a l
'launching' . . .

**But the getting there the 40 days in the wilderness of
waiting for vision - the agonies of wrenching it out right - the doubts & temptations of the devil(s) that beset
while all that struggle is in progress - the terror of the
mirror held up by one's own self up to one's broken nature - the poem miXing from a tape - a reel of life as
Tony McNeill puts it - the dub dub dub from one's own
self & test & question: IS THIS TRUE? the terrible wrestle
to convey the truth since there is always the temptati-
on/the seduction to allow the word to lead you on to
something else to falsify or make it easier on yrself or
because of pressure: mundane time or health, false sen**

se of destiny or deadline or that **distraction** like **destr uction** that **you** feared but **always can't refuse? to finish - CUT THE CORNER OF THE METAPHOR & get up** from the bitter cup - or like the student in the **Xam** room who can't deal wid it - fool himself - is hardly ever 'her' - that if he 'finish' early ... it might impresh the others

The 'Friends', I know, accused her of nourishing this 'dubiou talent': of too mu ch **giving in to 'Eddie'** as I am sure that you yrself have heard/ have said As if this made her **less,** as if indeed it made her **sick** - perhaps it even **kill** ed her. **YES THE POET KILL IM WIFE** An ole ole Story How she Sacrifice sheSelf (recall this being said of Colly's E and others too) She was more **You** than **She** etc etc etc This was part of the DotDot/DotDash burden & I think I have heard you w/ it too . . .

But she was my wife/the perfect poet's wife - I mean the perfect wife of/for the poet. She made it possible. Created from the very start & kept it go/ing to the last moments of her very life . the perfect temperature & space for the poems to be/come But she was also, as Edna Manley wrote to me, my very very **friend** & in this I am also blessed & lucky too beyond my knowing & **there- fore** as Edna also said [and AJ too] all the more too hard to bear to overstand re/cover from . . . but who care if i-man never write another word another poem . . .

# VIII

'THIS

BEIɊ

BUSINESS'

rt along my spine in the small of my ba

ck & weighing down upon my shoulders

& literally pushing me down Once I

had to get up & put on my shirt while

typing For there was like something or

some/one standing behind me/ & it was

making the very tiny hairs I didn't even

know I had along my spine sing softly

upwards like soft ants or gentle jesus

breezes like some/thing infinite  - that's

all I can say about it/ until it reach my

neck & up into my head so that the hai

(r) upon the bloodstream of my skull (for

I was very conscious of my skull like it was

staring) felt rushed up dark & heavy ta

ngled up like something boiling made of

snakes or something curled & uncoiling

& I cd hardly breathe & even now to wr

ite this brings it back to me/ until I noti

ced that there was a glass-front picture

up behind me & you know what people

say bout mirrors & how they shd be cov

ered from the saints or gods or ghosts or
deads w/ a blue cowl or cloth etc etc etc/
so that when I took the picture down things seemed much 'better' after that But
twice it was so bad I came back down
[to town] quite tired out

## 2

The first time I went up there af
ter she died, there was this smell of cocoa - before in fact I ask
ed Jean to make me some! (And
as it turned out there was no cocoa
left in that deserted silent house-
hold)

Next time there was the fright-
ful smell/ vv strong/ of a strange
cheap talc. Very sweet & fetid &
oppressive. Like the kind of pow

der you wd place upon a corpse
- somehow - a smell like from
the grave or something different like that. And I hear how
she was telling Miss Mac that
she didn't like the powder she
was using at Gib Camp Rd & told
me that when I went up [to IT] I
shd bring down her powder for
her - the talc she liked she used
And I wondered about that And
last night searching through pa
pers in the study there was the
distinct smell of coffee - before I
came across an envelope mar
ked **Coffee Board**

And even as I type this now during this passage of the tale th
ere is a faint whiff of (?more plea
sant) power/ but a presence/ here
/right now/ **again** And of course

from time to time wherever I go wherever I am ... **the odour of Miss
Mac's sulphur** ... the dirty-looking
fistfulls brought up here & lit & placed in tins in every corner of the
house/ to burn her out as if she
was in hell . One piece 'get way' &
seared a blk hole of calcutta in the
bedroom carpet And Jean say how I
muss repaint the house & change th
(e) furniture around **so she cyaaa
(n) recognize the place** - *my love
my life my darling Mexican!* - *your hou
se your care your love your home alway
(s) your smile of welcome* - and I shd
beat the bedding up & 'turn the ma
ttrass' & doan sleep in that bed Dr
Bratwaite and mek yu get some red
**underwears** fe wear - if not - *if not
what Jean?* - she go come back to
you for sex since she is still a woman & yr wife

163

And what's so cruel & fantastic & te

rrible in all this is that as poet & te

acher & researcher inna fe-we cultur

(e) - this is Xactly what you read &

hear - so that I was dispose - I was

suppose - you see - to - to believe

- if not believe in it - which is wh

(y) I went along w/ Miss Mac's sul-

phur in the first place And one mid

day sitting in the kitchen listening

to Jean - we heard these angry stam

ping footsteps on the floor above/up

stairs & w/ my hair going up & up

again & the back of my neck gone

snake we hear the footsteps stamp-

ing down the stairs towards us And

not a friend or soul up here or anywher

(e) to help me help me help me help me -

not a soul or relative or family or friend

- and all I wanted was some company

# 3

But the hardest part is that this really killing Me𝒳ican convertin (g) her to images that I refuse to name but are already here - eye-corner in the shadows of thi (s) house of almost-silences - & like how Joan Haughton tell me that on every anniversary of his death, her father comes to her & her twin/triplet sisters in the flit ing format of a bat & Mary wo ndering if the crowd of flying ants that came into her house soon after Zea died in there . . . were messengers . . . 'the

# Cloud of Witnes ses'

For it can happen . in the dark night of the soul . w/ the folk questions worries admonitions .

165

she was not satisfy . she wa

(s) not satisfy . she was not

satisfy you was not there .

you did not take her in/to

'her own house' [on campus] as

you had promised her before

she died . and why was that

miraculous smile that had appe-

ared upon her lips after she di

ed & after you had placed the

adinkra on her /why was that

**smile** no longer there wh

en they brought her into the

chapel on that Monday after

noon [some say it was still there - but

it had GONE] & of course my questio

(n) my perhaps belief that there is

life after 'the depart'/ but what kind

what kind of

life/connection/communication

how & for how long etc etc etc & that every sin/gle thing you do affect
(s) yr dead helps them like some st
range midwife into new loveliness &
happiness & peace or stuns them do
wn still further into ugliness & restlessness & really death

& isn't this why you place cyandles like you do against the dark/ so that the new sightless might not lose th
eir way? and why you talk about a cloud of witnesses?

IX

# Letters
## to
# MaryMorgan

$$\text{I}_\text{n all cultures,}$$

in this day & age, I shd have thought, there are

ceritain customs connected w/ family

SUPPORT & community SUPPORT & LIFE/

not DEATH support/ helping towards the light

if not ensuring continuity and making it

possible, surely, for the blood to flow again thru

the tissue where there are **BLACK HOLES** &

deep deep caverns/scars

But it seems to me that we have

so marginalized our males (or have they so

marginalized them-

selves) that we don't even know **how** to

comfort them **X**cept perhaps as lovers or

chilldren . . . or in other words unless they

**SURRENDER** their pain & abasement to yr

**conditions** . . .


I mean widows we know how to deal with 'in

the culture'/ & they seem to know only too well

(if I may say so) how to signal for **HELP**/ how to

ensure/ even **ensnare** protec-

tion/reconstruction

- & I cannot mean any of this unkindly -

& in anycase they are usually more

physically& mentally prepared & independent

& have steadied themselves somehow for these

'eventualities' -

I mean at least they know how to shop inside

the  market or the supermarket/ how best to

feed themselves & others

sew buttons on etc etc etc/ or so it seems




## 2

But the widow's Other? *the widower?* in a-we-

culture? Depending on his age/con- dition he's

either useless cock or hot new  une**X**pected

'property'/ the newly 'eligible "bachelor"'. In

either/neither case

**NO**/**BODY** bizness wid im grief &

dislocation . im is suppose to **cope**

(*'real man' na cry*  etc etc etc)/

**& stann up pun im one two feets**

as VP rather harshly told me when I ask for

help

**3**

PS

As a nonJamaican 'Jamaican'/foreign na

tive/ resident/ nonresident alien or vice

versa verso ( not sure how this go ) be—

reft of wife ( dead wife ) & ( living ) sister w/

few real frenns ( I see this now )/


**outsider** ( it wasn't that before but

that's it now/ at least that's how I feel ) livin

up here in this what to the villagers *( o*

*let me stare far away from this one now )* can on

ly appear as Grudgeful Great House ( ou

( r ) lovely ole & rambling beat-up [& since

Sept ( again! ) 88 *ruined]* Maroon 'Dump' )/ I am

a double outer/ at this time when i need o

how i need so much the opposite  But perha

ps the saving grace of this — shall we

say — aspect of our culture — I begin to

suspect now — was [do I believe this?] lost

upon **The Middle Passage** — but not th

at first one from the golden coast & co

176

st of Guinea but this still salter one that I/we on today – that cut us from th
(e) tubes of yam & village/ into the her
ban *dancehall* & the dungle & the tides
of garbage & the garbage dump or as
Dream Chad puts it, from countryside &
buttapan on/to this Middle Classage Passage into 'dish' & 'dis'/ dis/str
ess dis/crimination the lack & lost of but
terflies & green & trees/ so that when
dark comes we never know again how
HELP can HELP . despite the flags/ &
?faith in a-we culture

## 4

**No - the dyam food int import-**
**ant - but you place a plate a**
**warm-up rice before me without**
**lookin at me - without speakin**
**to me - without my askin for it**

177

**- wantin it - as if i was some kind α heg or beggar or α cat or puppy - happy & 𝒳pectant of & for such mercies for such crumb-les**

**No - the dyam food int import-ant even when α hungry; but as α say before it is the kind & kin da word - the thoughtful act - the spiritual sup & sip together - the ingather - the partake - the share**

And yesterday, after Nev's funeral, there was a lot of touching & unspoken hand-grips even hugs But after that each one went him or her own way [like happened to me after Mex's death] despite the 'What can we do?' 'How can we help? but being careful really not to ask or not to mean the ask, avoid the eyes, or if the really ask, cringing away in shale or shallow/shadow or duckin down the pretend head in case me *really* ask in case me *really* answer . . .

**5**

Everyone, I feel, shd have - need
(s) - α Holy Family & α Circle of
Friends - no matter how few - α-
round which all is centred

And once upon α time, it feels, I
had this Family & such (what I
thought) α perfect Circle in which I loved felt *privileged* to be
so loved & webbed & was - I must have fooled myself? - much loved

You - αt this time of crisis - of
Χtremis - of the wild/erness - have condemned & drowned me to
this letter to these litters to help
less long long-distance telephone
(s) to gusts of grief & questions

For ever since that midnight birthday when she died & you met
me at the door with **She's Gone**
& sat down near me for a little
on the settee & so briefly briefly
touched me, there has been noth
ing else. No word. Not even little
sound. As if the whole wound ne
ver happened. As if she hadn't
even lived & was yr sister as if
she didn't dead in where you live & me yr brother

Is it that God perhaps thru you
& the silence of the 'Friends' (wh-
o when they - seldom - see me, don't
even call her name) is testing testing testing perhaps pushing per
haps punishing yr brother? To
take our Mother in one year &
in the next my Wife - the very
marrows narrows of my life & lo

180

ve choked out w/ sulphur - my
future - what that's worth - en-
trusted too much to the mercy &
'kindness of Strangers'? **Who
judges who? And how?**


# 6

[this reaches to the top of p18 of the second ms of the **Letters**
which goes on for three pages more but will end this ts here
in the hope that this has been a faithful record, over several
days, of what I felt at this crucial cross & crossage of my life:
the sense of being buked/ abandoned by my loved ones: sister,
family & friends -


i mean not even one [till Dream Chad came] to offer lil 'domestic hints'
like how long shd a pound of sugar last/ where do you find dog food
inside the supermarket/ what is this thing call Cremo. And even after
Dream Chad come - perhaps BECAUSE the Dream Chad come - you & wh
at I can only call 'the formerFriends' - get even more 'unculture'/what I
now almost calling ' johncrow culture' - as if because she blk & poor it

mean she dawg & slave & wrong & even sin perhaps & certainly no 'sis-er' to any of the 'middle classage sisters' So dat we both get shut-out in dis darkness of reduce/neglect And all that I have ever write & earn & learn go slidin down de mountain of dis world wid weed & wither = wid-ower. And I have ?lived to hear a 'formerFriend' (male gender this one time) tell me (thru me phone) that w/ she Dead i am now Nothing And yet another Friendship thanking me for HELP in 'days gone by' it seems said that I wd have (I get this right?) to collect the bread I cast upon her waters/ from somehow other waters But what I fear/fear for is not the fu-ture me/ but future of the poems As if dem want to write this writer off As if I-scribe become somehow dyem SCRIPT dyem scrawl & scribble cross de wall]

But I remember that as the light da
wned on that first morning of this sec
tion of the Diary & I heard the bird
(s) & saw the ground-doves on the l-
awn as the sun came up over the

182

mts & through the branches of yr

almond tree & as I remember the wor

ds of AJ & Sunitha & Bob Stewart . .

from so so far far now it seems [AJ

has gone (Xmas 89) - and Bob -  do you

know that **4** years after you write th-

at poem of the ring **4** gunman come o-

ne night in here where they had murda

**4** not long before & gagg me up & tie

me up & throw me down upon mi sleep li

ke any sack a dirty clothes & **wrench**

that lifeline love from off me flinger

# *('Is this gole, bwoy?')* ]

And I look out look up & hope that so-

me/where some/time here there will be pe-

ace & love/ **real peace & really love;**

that hearts will hurt no more the blood

not struggle always in the way it did &

that the meaning of these things these

**mysteries** I sometimes have to call them   - the loss the pain the absence like

an abscess or abyss the questions ques-

tions questions the problems problems pr

oblems may be one day resolved if not

revealed If not may I at least make like

a dove upon yr lawn my heart in patien

ce for this while/ begin to learn 'domest-

ic' & the other 'skills' .  blessing those St

rangers the NewFriends who have come

w/ help/


seeking the still waters w/ the knowledge

dearest sister, that whateverelse or what

- I love you. -


and remember was yr home we turned to

wards & gathered strength & certainty &

peace within its safe & cool & comfort &

that you made this possible - you we

re there - so that she did not die disc-

onsole on the street or propped up on th

(e) soft or lumpy pillows of a stranger

or in the muted disinfectant hulls of the

hospitals that she hated -


and so I hope that perhaps long after I

have written this . . . & ridden these ev-

ents . . . you will be walking back acro-

ss this broken ground towards me . . .

*X*

# EPIGRAPH

written by EKB just before the Mona Chapel Service
## 15 September 86
and read for EKB by Edward Baugh at that Service &  inserted by EKB into
her EKB  Bibliography published by Savacou as a memorial to her
## 15 October 86

/b/b

takes one look at this irie dahta of Guyana then visiting
Barbados April 1960 and married her by May.  She trekked with
me to Ghana of that year, whirling, I remember well, in a
blizzard of golden bees near Navrongo: **dash-way the
headtie,** a passing herdsman yelled: the cloth around her head
was damp with moisture in that desert; the thirsty buzzings
needed it/ climbing the sun/day morning Morne to look out over
Castries harbour, past Vigie Point &   Gros Islet through
harmattan to Martinique & Dominique & beyond to
Gorée, Senegal/
on ship deck dawn, watching
the unexpected rise/ Jamaica's awesome mountains blue
& pink & pearl that morning out of creation's liquid pebble
water 1962/ read sheet by sheet the miracle of **Rights of
Passage** in that Runaway Bay cabin during those white hot sea
& summer-diving days of 1965 near where Columbus landed/
near where that Daughter of the Dust came walking on the desert
water & all the poems she inspired after that/ helped found the
Caribbean Artists Movement (CAM) in London 1966; had time to
ride her motorbike through all that surf & London traffic strife,
buy a piano, play it, type my thesis, paint, travel, study, bring
up our son/shine Michael Kwesi

builds a fantastic house & home at Irish Tn
cutlass & waterboots/ the off-white Panama from Cuba coming
up the IT terraces
help start again the Citizens Association there, small coffee
ground along the slopes of Penlyne Castle facing Blue Mountain
smoke .  breaks into computers long before the current craze,
sets up the Tourist Board's new lovely library, and all the while
runs **Savacou** & me/ incessant stalks & arguments over a

poem's meaning(s) & with all this & more - so so much more -
remains so young & beautiful & gentle/ generous & therefore
unpretentious/ unassuming **canscious,** as we say, without
appearing too much so & with a **conscience** made so strong so
strong & I repeat so generous that it is **caritas** & always time
for friends & all the names of trees & plants & flowers at her
fingertips (so very rare in Caribbean people)
& with all my imperfections on her head, sometimes my sword
& shining shield & buckler, still able to maintain that subtile
temperature of love & peace & space to make the work here
listed possible & I must hope
enduring
[this is ref to her Bibliography EKB: his published prose & poetry 1948-1986]


To her, then,
Queen & Keeper of our modern Caribbean literature
- one of them, surely -
I call her out

not that she wd accept such grand description
- *if she'd seen this she'd take it out* -
but that is what she was & is from one who knows the grace that
God bestowed upon her to her very eyes & wonders from what
mud & leaf & twinkle coastland/forest/hinterland of drowned
Guyanas & the broeken Carib's Caribbean Sea
such delicate vibration of creation come & now give thanks for
having shared one little fragment of her giving living loving life

# XI

# THE TULIP TREE

The tree planting (there were some scares & breakdown hitches) after all went well, thank God. Started off, as you might xpect, feeling v upset Went first for the poor tree which had languished all night in the cold (one of the problems/hitches) then passed for Bev who said she'd planned to go up anyway to help out Jean which was good news Halfway up she realized that no one had remembered to invite Miss Mac which put a further dampner on my mind but didn't wish to turn the clock back clock back for her since it was already almost 7 and I wanted that the 'ceremony' begin by 8. In the end, Mary, who didn't reach till almost 8 (!) agreed to go back down w/ Gerry Craig but we decided finally that since now [almost] 'everyone' was there we'd better not delay anymore since it wd take some one hour before Mary cd return & besides Miss Mac might have gone off to Mass or something & there was the hope that since she & Kitty went to the same church, she might (I hoped!) turn up w/ Kitty & GBeck (though she didn't)

We began by opening the box w/ the ashes. Mary Aunt May Sola nge Bärbel & myself in Michael's room (the room w/the big free table - the 'computer room') Bärbel opened the box (I couldn't) - a thin 8-inch

mahogany affair w/a sliding cover & there were the ashes in this plastic bag (Mrs Clarke had told me/warned me - *'urns no longer imported'* - though y-
ou cd get a plastic imitation . . . )

There was plenty of ash & the box that contained it was quite
heavy with it but it wasn't wood-ash-white but a kind of (I was
surprised) pink/brown w/ white flecks in it - like coral sand w/ little
clips of fingernails of shells & conchs & perhaps crab in there -
that smooth & shine & hint of pink: the sand of sea & time our or-
igins But a little larger & sharper & grittier than sand which really has been rolled around by whale & wheel of wave & plankton

We poured the ash into a container, a kind of small blue /bronze-
like looking ewer found by Jean in one of our cupboards & prob
brought by us from India but this was so small that we had to get a
second vessel & even then almost half the ash was left/was this my
loved one's body?

One Irish Tn lady who also was surprised the ashes were not white -
she had been curious to see it/see them - dressed in her white &white tie-
head - all ready for her Zion Church much higher up the morning,
said it was wicked, this burning of the body, and did she ask for that . . .?

198

$S$ome is to go to Guyana, some to Barbados, a little I've decided to keep The rest I think I'll pour into her garden spot [in the end we poured that 'little' third into the planting of her tulip tree] & when I was going downstairs to get the second vessel, I put some of the ashes on my tongue & swallowed her


$B$ut before we even touched her earth, we stood in silence for a moment (Mary, Aunt May, Solange, Bärbel, me) w/all the others knowing nothing / talking outside the window. Then Bärbel said a prayer After which, on instinct, I touched the ashes w/ my middle-finger fingertip & placed what was stuck there upon the forehead, like a **tika**, of the four, embracing each one each in turn as I did this. Then it was poured into the IT vessels, Bärbel said another prayer, and we went down to join the others $><$ then down the garden steps to the lawn of $X$osa grass & then another flight of steps down to the wider lower terrace where Harry had cut down the kidney mango tree that had been there & had earlier that morning dug a hole quite deep (like a round grave, somehow, as if we were burying after all) where Sidrak's tulip tree, stripped of its leaves, was waiting

Lynette had brought two rose plants also: one she called **Peace** (white) the other **Touch of Class** (a coral pink) which people said was very propriate - *'very Doris'*, Hazel Campbell said - & Gerry [Cr aig] suggested that we plant them near the tulip future

I asked Mrs Hamilton, as so usual up in Irish Tn, to take charge of the proceedings (again there was a large IT turn-out though I had invited only a few!/ forgot Mrs Mais so of course she didn't come which I'm v sorry about [she too has died /Ap 92/ since I wrote this] & Mr Jonas didn't make it/prob couldn't w/ his *pressure* & the strain upon the body coming down our hill) & there was like graveside hymn-singing from the Irish Tns (most of them had brought hymn-books & Bibles/some on their way to church) & Mrs H read from **Corinthians** (D's 'Charity' again) and Bärbel spoke & prayed, pointing out that Mexican had now become part of the IT landscape that she loved & in this way she wd - as long as world was here - be with me/ with us always

& then, unexpectedly, Mr Ɍeid, the 'likkle man' wh (o) always came down from up his hill to visit Me χican, who often helped him w/ his sick wife (car lifts etc - it was his grandchild w/ the bums I'd taken do wn that rainy May) & who wd come from time to time to help her plant out yam or chocho, calalloo or skellion, peas - or just come down to find out how she was [he too has died [Oct 92] - face downwards in a gully near our place after one whole day and a night they cannot find him - it was this same grand-daughter of the burns next morning saw his cap/ to find him. . .]

This Mr Reid - Mass Phillip son of Mass Hall, D's first firm friend up here - bedridden now - his own wife blind - we never imagining that she wd go before him in this way! - had been invi-ted to the Tulip Tree & he had come down punct-ual in good time as usual w/ his quick soft anxi-ous step, 'calling to the House' as was his wont & went down right away to the spot where Harry ha (d) been digging & where the tree wd be & even while everybodyelse was chatting in the house or on the upper level of the garden was, down beside the new-made hole, alone, looking out across the landscape - across the valley out to Kingston & the sea - like, as Bärbel noticed/ said - some kind of sentinel - she caught a lovely photograph of him like that - and though I didn't recognize him then - we so so seldom

201

dol -

# ELUEGGBA

**god of the pathways -**

So that when we thought it was all over - prayers sai

(d) hymns sung the obsequies properly performed 'trad-

itionals' observed the tulip tree in place - though some-

thing was I still felt missing -


Mass Reid began to sing at first it was like talking & the whole

thing was so intimate it was like talking to himself & Mexican &

me and then to all of us & from us to the trees & wind & grass &

then the hillslope where she/her her ashes were becoming w/ the

sky its blue so very blue that morning & with God & with the God

in all of this in all of us circle through circle through cycle through

time

•

beginning

•

**Lord**

**watch between I & you/when we is absent one from**

**one another**

& as he
## worked

because it was this too

he was like washing the grass of its dirt between his palms &

letting it drip drip drip onto the new planted tree from his

fingers/sing/talking to Mex & to God & to himself & to all of us &

sometimes sighing from deep down from where his song was coming

deep deep down & frayed out into his throat & through his teeth

like carrot root or beet or yampe


**I never meet you in person**

# = this could have only
# been to God =

&

there were these silences as if he was

**listening**

then


**O Mrs Brathwaite**


hands working all the while, the earth being gently patted like a

comfort reassurance since it was now  her body


**such a lovely person**


&

h e

**shook**

the  tree


**such a peaceful person**


&

h e

**shook**

the  tree

the dirt coming away from the clods & grass & falling into that

gentle moment & the whole place silent & we like gone away

forever monument

w/ wherever he was travelling & he slow & deliberate the voice

now low intense & intimate

•

**I love her like I love mi own wife**

**. . . and I told you so Mr Brathwaite**

**. . . so beautiful . . .**

the voice muttering down like a dark wick now between speech &

song & the hands

working working working working

all the while washing the grass releasing its dirt smoothing the

rough & now his fingers **flicked** the planted stalk

**Rest now**

**alright**

. . . is alright now . . .


Watch . . . I & you


Watch . . . between I & you


&

suddenly as an end & signal he plucked the whole green stem w/ his fin-

gers & it vibrated there in the sunlight like music like the string of life it

had become


**ahhhhhhhhhhhhhhhhhhhhhhhhhhhhhh Mrs Brathwaite**

&

for a little while longer the

**m m m m m m m m m m m m m m m m m m m m m m m m m m m m m**

of the song of his voice in the Irish Tn light

a clear day coming up a blue day

a quiet quiet quiet morning & the brief thousand rising suns in the

mahogany tree's dark halfway down the slope


206

her stem

# singing

# XII

# ANYANEANYANE
## THE AWAKENING

One late afternoon I drove Aunt May &
Dream Chad up to Hardwar Gap & the
Park up there Looking across from where
we were there was a valley & beyond that
on the same level w/ us a wood in mist &
you cd see a road & the light under the
trees in the distance but it was like over
there & you couldnt see the connection
how it got where it was how you cd get
there & there was no one over there Only
peace As if **there** was where she was walking away from us but perhaps waiting but
each day getting more & more distance &
getting more & more involve w/ what was
happening over there & meeting the people out there & getting to know them &
her Mother eventually getting the news
that she had arrived & setting out to find
her in that landscape over there so near so
far far away in the grey green going-down
evening sun forever & for ever Heartease

Which is where she is/in that soft distance shining & I was suddenly & at last happy & very very sad & lonely at the same
time because she felt so lonely too but some how at peace & there was nothing I cd
do nothing nothing I cd do anymore nothing I cd ever do ever & ever again but to
lose her there & that way where I cd see
her & not see her beyond that valley high
up there in the Blue Mountains

*Wisconsin Studies in American Autobiography*

WILLIAM L. ANDREWS
General Editor

Robert F. Sayre
*The Examined Self: Benjamin Franklin, Henry Adams, Henry James*

Daniel B. Shea
*Spiritual Autobiography in Early America*

Lois Mark Stalvey
*The Education of a WASP*

Margaret Sams
*Forbidden Family: A Wartime Memoir of the Philippines, 1941–1945*
Edited, with an introduction, by Lynn Z. Bloom

*Journeys in New Worlds: Early American Women's Narratives*
Edited by William L. Andrews

Mark Twain
*Mark Twain's Own Autobiography:*
*The Chapters from the* North American Review
Edited, with an introduction, by Michael J. Kiskis

*American Autobiography: Retrospect and Prospect*
Edited by Paul John Eakin

Charlotte Perkins Gilman
*The Living of Charlotte Perkins Gilman: An Autobiography*
Introduction by Ann J. Lane

Caroline Seabury
*The Diary of Caroline Seabury: 1854–1863*
Edited, with an introduction, by Suzanne L. Bunkers

Cornelia Peake McDonald
*A Woman's Civil War: A Diary with Reminiscences of the War,*
*from March 1862*
Edited, with an introduction, by Minrose G. Gwin

Marian Anderson
*My Lord, What a Morning*
Introduction by Nellie Y. McKay

*American Women's Autobiography: Fea(s)ts of Memory*
Edited by Margo Culley

Frank Marshall Davis
*Livin' the Blues: Memoirs of a Black Journalist and Poet*
Edited, with an introduction, by John Edgar Tidwell

Joanne Jacobson
*Authority and Alliance in the Letters of Henry Adams*

Kamau Brathwaite
*The Zea Mexican Diary*
Foreword by Sandra Pouchet Paquet